The Great Blue Hills *of* God

The Great Blue Hills *of* God

A Story of Facing Loss, Finding Peace,
and Learning the True Meaning of Home

Kreis Beall

CO-FOUNDER OF BLACKBERRY FARM

CONVERGENT NEW YORK

Published in the United States by Convergent Books, an imprint of Random House, a division of Penguin Random House LLC, New York.

CONVERGENT BOOKS is a registered trademark and its C colophon is a trademark of Penguin Random House LLC.

Grateful acknowledgment is made to Zachry K. Douglas for permission to reprint the poem "The Broken," originally self-published in the collection *More Soul Than Human,* copyright © 2014 by Zachry K. Douglas. Used by permission of Zachry K. Douglas. All right reserved.

Library of Congress Cataloging-in-Publication Data
Names: Beall, Kreis, author. | Blackberry Farm (Walland, Tenn.)
Title: The great blue hills of god : from the founder of Blackberry Farm, a story of enormous success, unfathomable loss, and discovering the true meaning of home / Kreis Beall.
Identifiers: LCCN 2019021508 (print) | LCCN 2019980744 (ebook) | ISBN 9781984822246 (hardcover) | ISBN 9781984822253 (ebook)
Subjects: LCSH: Beall, Kreis. | Blackberry Farm (Walland, Tenn.) | Farmers—Tennessee—Biography. | Farm life—Tennessee—Biography.
Classification: LCC S417.B34 A3 2019 (print) | LCC S417.B34 (ebook) | DDC 630.9768—dc23
LC record available at https://lccn.loc.gov/2019021508
LC ebook record available at https://lccn.loc.gov/2019980744

Printed in Canada on acid-free paper

convergentbooks.com

10 9 8 7 6 5 4 3 2 1

First Edition

Book design by Diane Hobbing

To Mom, Mammy, Mary Anne—the three most important women in my life. Everything I am and know, I owe to you.

CONTENTS

The Great Blue Hills *of* God

Chapter 1

BREAKING

Most women of my "certain age" line their walls or fill their shelves with photos of children and grandchildren—happy, gap-toothed smiles inside glossy frames. For years, my walls were hung with beautiful color photos and magazine spreads of my houses, each one unique, expertly decorated, and having its own given name: Hedgerose, Rose Bay, Maple Cottage, Toad Hall. I thought that the physical space, the walls, the paint, the rugs and windows, the way the chairs faced and how the side tables accented a room, the meals that came out of the kitchen—everything that made a house look great and feel great—were the building blocks of home. I believed all it took was organization, hard work, and planning.

Now all my plans had come undone. As I stood on the threshold of sixty, my marriage was over, I was disconnected from my sons, I spent too little meaningful time with my grandchildren.

To the outside world, I was the co-founder of one of the most idyllic spots on earth, Blackberry Farm. It was not a farm in the conventional sense of raising dairy cattle or crops. Rather, my husband, Sandy, and I had started with a dilapidated, 1940 low-ceiling house with eight guest rooms and grew it into a Relais & Châteaux estate and restaurant, a stylish, award-winning destination at the edge of Tennessee's Great Smoky Mountains. Its iconic views, the shimmering trees and hills, the white-painted rockers perched above a sweeping lawn, were routinely featured in glossy lifestyle and travel magazines. People began referring to it simply as "Blackberry."

Beyond Blackberry, I was known for my own cooking and entertaining, for being married to Sandy, founder of the Ruby Tuesday restaurant chain, and for my photogenic family and two successful sons. And I never dissuaded anyone, not even my mother, my sisters, or my closest friends, that this was my story until I could no longer paper over and pretend. Until I had no choice but to tell my truth.

I began by giving up what I had clung to the longest: my image of the perfect home. From a multi-bedroom house, I moved to a 324-square-foot farm shed on the edge of Blackberry—a space that not long before had been piled high with broken Christmas decorations that no one could quite commit to the rubbish bin. When I stepped into that single room, I left behind the cushion of things, an oversize closet, kitchen gadgets, a long dining table, and matched sets of comfy chairs. Suddenly unburdened of creature comforts and objects, I had no choice but to meet myself head-on.

If I wanted a view, I would have to step outside into whatever weather we were having and let my eyes rest on the mountains the Cherokee Indians had named the Great Blue Hills of God.

If I wanted a rush of cooling air, I would have to stand and breathe the morning fog rising from the creek or the clumps of heavy dew on the meadow. If I wanted people, I would have to intentionally seek them. If I wanted a project, the only available thing to be worked on was me, perhaps the hardest renovation of all.

But I could not begin to build a future until I found a new foundation on which to rebuild my life. It began with a prayer:

> *Heavenly Father,*
> *Grant me courage,*
> *Grant me wisdom*
> *To learn from the past*
> *And not be crippled by it.*
> *So that like Joseph, I may be a*
> *Blessing to my earthly family*
> *And the world at large.*
> *In Jesus' name,*
> *Amen.*

Starting with those words, I did something I had never done before: I told the truth to myself. I realized I had helped to create a place of flawless beauty, accolades, and daily perfection, Blackberry Farm, while living a life that was flawed. Now, I could finally see the scars. What I learned was that my real story was not the one I had expected. It's a story about success, yes, but also about tragedy and heartache. Ultimately, it is a story of deciding to consciously choose joy and live through pain, with a deep and abiding faith in God.

When I started on this journey, I did not know all the ways in which life could be hard and yet still be beautiful. I did not know that seeking forgiveness and finding God's fierce love would change so many things. I was still learning that home is not a physical place, but the space you make inside your heart. Only when I let go of perfectionism and learned to sit with devastation, and from there slowly breathe in meaning, did I discover that what I had built was not a picture-perfect life, but a real and beautiful one, stronger for the breaking.

Chapter 2

BEGINNINGS

I had two truths growing up: that I lived in the most beautifully decorated house in Knoxville, and that most mornings I could not wait to race out our front door.

The house was beautiful because of my mother. She selected the antique Heriz rugs that lay heavy on our floors. She hung rich crewel-embroidered drapery to accent our windows and chose the crushed burnt orange velvet upholstery that covered our sofa in the den. Rather than the painted porcelain figurines and colored glass so popular in Knoxville homes, she arranged blue and white Chinese ginger jars and Japanese Imari vases on our shelves and tabletops. In the 1950s, when everyone else was buying matched furniture store sets, Jane Bailey started collecting antiques, intricate secretaries and tall mahogany highboys. Those highboys were the furniture equivalent of Mom, so pretty to look at with their willowy lines, slender legs, and graceful motion. But it was my father, David Bailey, the ex–University of Tennessee linebacker and youngest football player to take the field during the 1945 Rose Bowl, whose outsized presence ruled our home.

My older sister, Keith, and I cannot clearly recall the basic details of our father's face from our childhood. I can picture his broad shoulders and balding head, his thick hands, the cut of his suits, his fedora hats, and his big legs, but when I try to envision his face, my mind draws a blank. Probably because when he spoke to us, my sister and I were always looking down.

Almost before we could walk, we learned to tiptoe around his fearsome temper. We told him exactly what he wanted to hear. If my mother wanted to do anything substantive, she did not dare ask; instead, she waited until my father was out of town.

David Bailey came by his meanness honestly. His own father, Lucien, was formidable. In downtown Knoxville, people would rather cross the street than walk next to him. At the Cherokee Country Club, he took pride in "whooping" his opponents on the golf course and making everyone from the caddies to the pros cringe. His end came on that golf course at the thirteenth hole. A few boys were shooting squirrels in the surrounding woods. One errant bullet spun through the trees and exited onto the fairway, following a near perfect trajectory to reach Lucien's brain.

Before he was shot, Lucien lived a big life, and behind that big life was big debt. At age twenty-six, my father assumed control of his father's investment firm and began working to pay off his many obligations. I'm not sure which man was angrier deep down, but I know my father was a better businessman. He ran a successful brokerage, started a water company, and in 1961 got into liquor distribution. One of his partners was my grandmother, my mother's mother, Hazel Kreis Oliver, where I got my name. We called her Mammy. In old photos, she looks pretty, but by the time I knew her, she was short and stout. Her face was permanently weathered and ruddy from running the family farm. Mammy never complained; she just tightened her lips into a thin line and kept going.

Mammy was about the only person David Bailey couldn't bully, though he tried. Among my most vivid childhood memories is the night Keith and I heard yelling and snuck out on the balcony that overlooked our den. We lay down, making ourselves small and flat, and watched Dad shout at Mammy. I have no memory of what the argument was about. Instead, what I see is the scene: Dad pulling himself up to his full six feet, two inches and bellowing at tiny Mammy, who silently held her ground.

I had seen my father yell at other people: the waitresses at Howard Johnson's when our food took too long, a cab driver in New York, when he grew so enraged as the man drove off that he kicked at the bright yellow door. But this was Mammy, who left her front door unlocked so I could bike over after school and make warm, buttered toast in her cool tile kitchen or swim in her bright Italian mosaic pool. Mammy, who let Keith and me charge to her account at Long's Drug Store so we could buy comic books, a cheeseburger, French fries, and a Coke, sit at the counter, eat, and read.

In that moment on the balcony, as my father's voice thundered below, I was truly terrified. I resolved to do whatever it took not to make him mad again.

The Bailey household was surprisingly short on formal rules and traditions, because neither my mother nor my father wanted to be bothered with creating or enforcing them. But we did have a rule that everyone must be seated at the table for breakfast and dinner, and at dinner, children had to eat their green vegetable. This was, however, the 1950s and '60s, when the freshest assortment of green vegetables was usually found in the supermarket's canned foods aisle. Week after week, my mother fixed Le Sueur canned peas. I would dutifully eat them or scrape them into my hand and hide them in my pocket when my parents weren't looking, the principle being that by the time the dishes were ready to be cleared, the peas had disappeared from my plate. But Keith refused. She wouldn't eat her peas, and she wouldn't put them in her pocket or the other desperate measure: smush them against the underside of the table. The continued presence of Keith's peas was unacceptable to our father. Night after night, he made her stay in her chair until she ate them. Only when our neighbor Jane told us to spread ketchup on everything did the pea standoff end.

Keith and I grew up as polar opposites, starting with the way we looked. She was dark-haired and sturdy, while I was blond and spectacularly average. I wasn't pretty, but I wasn't ugly. I had a crooked smile, but I wasn't self-conscious enough to be bothered by having to wear braces for nearly ten years to remake my jawline. I molded myself into the peaceful, passive daughter, thinking that being pleasant and nice would protect me from anything. For years, I liked to say that my motto was

"The answer is yes. What's the question?"

Keith had it harder. In sixth grade, her teacher, Mrs. Dowell, set up a scale in the hall outside of her classroom. Every student had to have his or her weight measured, and then their names and weights were posted outside their classroom doors, in a peculiar kind of early 1960s hazing and shaming. At five-six and 117 pounds, Keith was pronounced the heaviest in the school. She wasn't remotely heavy for her height and athleticism—she was a champion equestrian—but that didn't matter. The other kids nicknamed her Fatty.

We lived differently, fought differently, and when we weren't fighting, we usually avoided each other. We had the two upstairs rooms: hers was pink and smaller, mine was blue and larger. She had a double bed, I had two single beds, and we shared a Jack and Jill bathroom, which was the source of most of our fights, particularly who got to use the bathroom first. Keith was taller and stronger than me, so she could always win in a physical contest. I retaliated by being the sister who could win the verbal battle, stinging her with a hurtful word, a skill I honed by watching my father. After I spoke, I would, as Mom put it, "run like hell away." I knew Keith couldn't catch me.

About the only thing we were united on was our decidedly mixed view of a new sibling. When I was ten and Keith was twelve, our parents told us they had a surprise for us and asked us to guess what it was going to be. We spent an entire day debating. I was absolutely certain we were going to get a swimming pool. Keith was absolutely certain it was going to be a horse. Neither of us was prepared for the answer to be "a new baby."

Otherwise, our worlds rarely overlapped. When as sixty-something women we compared our high school memories, Keith paused and said, "I think you were a cheerleader," and she only remembered that because she once saw a photo of me in my uniform on Dad's desk. That obliviousness cut both ways. I recall going to only one of Keith's horse shows, although she competed in hundreds of them.

Despite my father's iron fist, Keith and I, and later our baby sister, Kim, whom we both came to love, grew up in a household dominated by women. My mother likes to say that she was an only child because of the Great Depression, but perhaps she was an only child because Mammy married so badly. Pappy was a mason when they met, but he stopped working after the banks failed. What he did instead was drink. Where my other grandfather was a functioning alcoholic who drank heavy each night and then got up, put on a three-piece suit, and went into the office, Pappy was what we called "a drunk-drunk." He went on benders, disappearing for days or weeks at a time, and leaving Mammy to run the dairy farm and hatchery alone. Before there was the phrase "working single mother" Mammy essentially was one. Hazel and Jane's regular mother-daughter outings were trips to Knoxville's Market Square, where they sold turkeys and chickens out of a booth.

As a child, I ate nearly every Sunday dinner at Mammy and Pappy's, but often Pappy's seat was empty. When he was gone, no one said a word. We just made the same small talk and passed the rolls, green beans, sweet potatoes, and pork roast. I never considered the DNA of flawed attachments that passed from Mammy to our mom and down to Keith and me.

My mother, Jane Bailey, was not like other mothers. Other mothers sported bouffant hairdos and wore wraparound skirts, while my mother's hair was styled in a sleek, short bob and she dressed her slender five-foot-eight frame in sharkskin pleated skirts and perfectly tailored chemises. She began her day not with a cup of coffee but with a bottle of Coca-Cola and a cigarette, from which she blew graceful, elongated smoke trails. Her age was always twenty-nine. When the *Knoxville News Sentinel* wrote her up in a feature story headlined "She Lives Fashion and Looks It," Mom admitted to owning at least sixteen pairs of "home pants," favoring toreadors and pedal pushers. The article began, "Jane Bailey (Mrs. David T.) is one of the few women who can wear knitted shorts and look like a dream walking away." The second sentence rattled off her "model" measurements of 35-24-34.

So much of Keith's and my childhood is captured in that yellowed newspaper clipping with a photograph of our elegant mother in a long, thin sheath and Keith and me in our matching little-girl sheath dresses, trying to hold ourselves in the same graceful poses. Neither of us succeeded, but I was smaller and more petite, and the instant the camera's shutter snapped, my mother's gaze was focused entirely on me and away from Keith, who looks helplessly at her back. Keith hated her peas and loved buttery rolls, and my mother would drive her to an endocrinologist in Atlanta to try to speed up her metabolism and lower her weight. I envied their trips—I thought they were exotic and fun. Keith dreaded them. And neither of us told the other.

Mom had been a New York runway model before she married. After her freshman year at the University of Tennessee, she convinced Mammy to let her move to Manhattan to attend art school, but she never enrolled. Instead, she took a taxi straight to the garment district. It was just after World War II, and the major modeling agencies were sandwiched next to each other on the same block. Mom was hired by the second agency she visited, not because she had a particular talent, but because she was the exact same size and measurements as its lead model, a woman named Adele. Clothes could be pinned and sewn to mom's frame, as if she were a mannequin, before Adele showed them off.

But Mom was determined to become a model. She watched and absorbed how they walked and their poses until she could move with the same grace and confidence, and the fashion houses' latest creations were being fitted for her to display. Then on a visit home to Tennessee, David Bailey took Mom on a date. He proposed soon after, and Mom left New York to be "a good Southern wife."

It never quite took. In all of Knoxville, the person Mom loved most was her hairdresser, Kristopher Kendrick. She called him "Brother," and they shared everything. Kristopher was married with five children, but beneath the facade, he was gay. My mother became his friend and business partner, first in a hair salon, where I remember the cold porcelain sink jutting uncomfortably into my little three-year-old neck when I had my hair washed, and later in a ladies' dress shop that they named Benjamin Jones. Even though he has been gone for years, she still refers to him, and not our father, as her "soulmate."

In our family universe, I was Mom's mini-me. I loved watching her eat tiny cream cheese and olive sandwiches while I ate miniature cinnamon toast. I happily tagged along when she went to the beauty salon, the clothing store, or the White Store, our local grocery chain, where I would observe every detail about the food displays or the other shoppers. She would let me prattle on for hours about what I had seen, while I wondered why she hadn't noticed things that seemed so vivid to me. When she left the house to model for Rich's Department Store or Sunday features in the newspaper, I would cry, "Please don't go to work," but she simply sailed off in her convertible, a chartreuse Impala with a white leather interior and matching top.

Over time, watching my mother, I absorbed her independence and can-do attitude. Once I found a large snake slithering on our basement steps, I screamed and froze. Mom came, glanced at the reptile, calmly got an ax, and severed its head with a single blow. When I was about four, she took Keith and me to the Tennessee Valley Authority Fair. Somehow I got separated in the thick crowd amid the rides and animals. Rather than stand still and cry, I walked straight up to a man and asked if I could ride on his shoulders to look for my mom. By the time I was six or seven, I was free to roam the neighborhood alone on my bike. I did not recognize it then, but I was cementing my life around having an easy exit strategy, a way out of any physical space or situation.

At home, we did not linger around the dinner table or sit together to watch television. We came together and then scattered. We lived parallel but disconnected lives. I became a fixture at the home of our next-door neighbors, the Townsends. I loved that their house was so predictable, unlike my own. Each afternoon, at 4:45, the four Townsend children took their baths, supervised by the housekeeper, and put on their footie pajamas. They ate dinner at 5:30 every night in the kitchen. Each weeknight had a set dinner; my favorite was Tuesday's boiled chicken and applesauce. Sometimes in the summers, we'd play outside after supper, the Townsends running around in their pajamas. They had a slide, which is where I fell and broke my front tooth. I ran and told my mother, and she said, "Let me see." I smiled, and she started crying. I kept repeating, "No, it doesn't hurt, Mommy. You don't have to cry." But of course, she wasn't crying about the pain; it was about my wrecked smile.

When I wasn't at the Townsends, I would visit Mr. and Mrs. Schubert, who lived on the other side of our house. Tall and thin, Mrs. Schubert looked like a Disney witch, with pale, nearly translucent skin, heavy black hair, and the two largest nostrils I had ever seen. We were Presbyterians, but the Schuberts were Baptists, and Mrs. Schubert kept a dry home. We would sit in her kitchen, chatting, and watch the red mercury in the glass barometer rise on sunny days or fall before a storm. Mr. Schubert was stocky and spent most of his time with his vast model train collection. Each night, like clockwork, I'd see him from my bedroom window walking around his backyard. I'd ask my mother what Mr. Schubert was doing outside, even in the winter, and my mother would reply, "Checking his garden," although his "garden" was nothing more than a piece of patchy lawn. No matter how often I asked, the answer was always the same. It was years before I knew that he went outside because he kept his liquor bottles buried in the ground.

That's how almost everything Southern goes. You don't say anything. Nobody's an alcoholic. Nobody's abusive. Nobody's having affairs, nobody's gay. Nobody's sad, or sick, or deaf. If you fry your chicken right, butter your beans, and put just enough sugar in the sweet tea, everything is good. If your hard, brittle Zoysia grass looks too brown in the winter, like Mrs. Long's on the corner of Kenesaw and Keowee Street, then you just pay your lawn man to spray-paint your front yard a bright spring green.

I was guilty of it, too. I believed that "Yes" was the one, reliable answer that would make everything fine.

But sometimes it is the question that matters most of all.

Chapter 3

SANDY

Sandy Beall wasn't introduced to me; I introduced myself to him. It turned out to be my first big interview, and I didn't even know that I was being considered for a position.

While he was in college at the University of Tennessee, Sandy had opened a restaurant named Ruby Tuesday. Now, three years later, Ruby Tuesday had three locations and was about to launch its fourth in Gatlinburg, Tennessee; it was officially a chain. My friend Pat was desperate to go to the opening, not because she wanted anything on the menu, but because she wanted to date the restaurant's new assistant manager. "Well, let's go," I said. She looked slightly horrified and said, "We can't. We're not invited." I just smiled and said, "That's no problem. They're not going to kick us out. It's okay." I was convincing enough that she got in the car and we drove the hour and twenty minutes to Gatlinburg.

*   *   *

I wasn't worried because while on paper Knoxville is a city, it operates as a small town. I knew Sandy Beall the way that many Southerners know their mom's best friend's cousin's nephew. For years, I had seen the Beall family at church on Christmas and Easter, and his mom and my father's sister had been childhood friends. To my twenty-two-year-old mind, that was enough of a connection to just walk in.

There were no fireworks when we shook hands. We said hi, and Sandy invited us to his house for another party after the opening. I went to help Pat in her quest for a date. Sandy never showed up. We left and I didn't give Sandy Beall another thought.

At the time, I was taking an evening typing class. I had graduated from Tulane University with an art history degree, which qualified me to do absolutely nothing except work at a museum like the Metropolitan in New York, and I couldn't have gotten a job there if I'd tried. Instead, I enrolled in paralegal school in Atlanta. In 1974 in the South, being a paralegal was a new profession. I went to school for three months and came home to Knoxville as a paralegal who did not know how to type.

My parents were friends with Senator Howard Baker and his wife, Joy, and that, along with my college degree and new paralegal skills, helped me land an internship in Senator Baker's Washington office. But the internship didn't start until the summer, and I had six months in Knoxville to fill. I went to see an administrator at the University of Tennessee's legal aid society and told him I wanted to volunteer as a paralegal. His response was "What's that?" I gave him my best definition of the job that also happened to fit me: "A paralegal is an assistant who cannot type." He made me a criminal paralegal, working with some of the most vulnerable people in Knoxville, and I had visions of Perry Mason, helping the unjustly accused go free.

So in the spring of 1975, I was volunteering, waiting for my Senate internship and my move to Washington, D.C., and taking a typing class. What few rules there were, I mostly followed, but I had no overarching plans for "what would come next."

I was working on a Monday morning when my phone rang. It was Sandy Beall. He had tracked me down through a friend, gotten my number, and was calling to ask me out. As luck would have it, my car was in the shop and I needed a ride home. A date seemed particularly convenient, so I asked Sandy to pick me up after typing class. He rolled up in his silver Jaguar with two cut-crystal highball glasses filled with icy gin and tonic waiting on the dashboard. I was a girl who didn't really drink or go on dates with boys in fancy cars. It was as if I had stepped into a scene straight from a Hollywood romance. In my ugly brown corduroy skirt, I felt special and sophisticated and more than a little smitten. Sandy felt it, too. After that, we saw each other nearly every night. I was enveloped by Sandy Beall.

Sandy wasn't handsome in the traditional sense. He was short and had the beginnings of a belly, with a soft face, blond hair, and a terrible-looking scraggly beard. But he was confident with an enthusiasm for life that practically radiated off of him. Our relationship wasn't a "sweep me off my feet" type of attraction. I was never terrified that my world would implode if I did not have him. Rather, I saw a man who was self-assured, directed, and didn't depend on me to fulfill some emotional void. And I thought that perhaps I would never meet anyone quite like this again.

I fell in love with Sandy's energy and his ability to answer a question without the slightest hesitation. Sandy Beall has probably never uttered the words "I don't know" when it comes to making a decision. He never left any doubt that he knew what he was talking about; no one had time to consider the possibility he might be wrong or improvising. He was that fast. With Sandy, I felt like I was standing on a precipice, but the plunge would be exhilarating; we could jump off at any time, parachutes deployed, and glide our way to the next grand adventure.

I proposed to him two weeks after we met, which was hardly romantic and highly impulsive. It was a matter of logistics. Since we had started dating, I had fallen asleep at his house nearly every night. We would wake up in each other's arms, and soon thereafter, my panic would set in. I had to get home before my father knew I was gone—I was still terrified of him. So I looked at Sandy one night and said, "Listen, if we are going to continue with this routine, we should probably just go ahead and get married." He answered, "Okay." We took another two weeks to consider the proposition and determine that it was in fact a good idea. Four weeks from introductions to engagement. But no one ever said, "What are you thinking?" Least of all us.

Our marriage, I would come to understand, was built like those old, double-sided partners' desks, with two separate sides, separate drawers, and a clear division of decisions and labor. It was a highly successful pairing of two independent human beings.

Sandy offered to get me an engagement ring, but I said no. Instead, I told him that whenever we could afford it, I wanted a pool so I could swim. During college, I had grown to love the repetitive, mind-clearing motion of swimming laps, and I imagined walking out to my own backyard in the mornings and diving in. Sandy, being Sandy, didn't flinch, he simply said okay.

We got married four months after we met, scheduled in between Ruby Tuesday restaurant openings. Sandy was planning and opening new locations so quickly that I hardly saw him. A friend offered to throw us a Great Gatsby engagement party, complete with period costumes and old cars, I went to a men's shop, M.S. McClellan's, and bought Sandy a white linen suit, a pink shirt, and flat cap made of white linen, so that he'd look like Jay Gatsby. I charged it to his account and didn't think anything of it. I didn't even consider whether he had enough in the bank to pay the bill. If he didn't, Sandy never said a word.

Our wedding day was flawless and completely over the top because I let my mother plan the entire thing. Keith had already gotten married, but there had been no wedding. She and her boyfriend, Jack, had eloped in neighboring Maryville. I was in college at the time and didn't even know my sister was married until I came home. My wedding was my mother's chance to put on a beautiful show. I remember her saying, "What do you want to do for your wedding?" My answer was "Whatever you want. I want you to do it." She said something like "Come on," in her slightly husky, smoke tinged voice, and I replied, "No really, everything you do, I'll like. All I want is to pick out my dress. That's it." And that's all I did. She did everything else.

It was the one time my father was generous and happy to oblige; it no doubt helped that I was marrying so respectably. Sandy not only gave off the aura of success, but also came from a well-regarded Knoxville family. One of his friends made wedding T-shirts that read "The Great Merger." Sandy's father, Sam, was a top engineer at the U.S. government's Oak Ridge nuclear facility; he had worked on building the components of the atomic bomb that U.S. forces dropped on Japan to end World War II. Sandy's mother, Mary Anne, took care of their five children, played tennis, and was a prized member of the Junior League and Sequoyah Presbyterian, the church down the hill from my home. Almost every Sunday, the seven Bealls would march into church and take their seats in their preferred pew.

Now Sandy and I would be getting married in that church, where I used to color and doodle my way through Sunday school. When we went for our premarital consultation, Sandy's only request to the Reverend was that the actual service be as short as possible. He was very happy when at the rehearsal he discovered it had been whittled down to seventeen minutes, barely enough time to pledge the most basic vows. It was even more remarkable considering that we had twenty attendants to get up and down the aisle. All I remember was rounding a corner inside the church before the ceremony and seeing Sandy standing there, smiling, dressed in his elegant tails and clasping his bare hands. He had forgotten to bring his formal white rental gloves, while all his attendants had their gloves on.

Our reception was held at the Cherokee Country Club, and walking in, I felt completely in awe. My first thought was *Who are all these people?* Four parents had invited nearly eight hundred people. The receiving line took forever. Because I had abdicated the planning, I was as surprised as anyone to see how magically the club had been transformed. There were beautiful linens on every table, some of which belonged to my grandmother. Big columns ran along either side of the ballroom, and my mother had designed it so that swags of greenery were draped from end to end below the vaulted ceiling. Suspended at the center was a three-foot-tall classic antique brass birdcage, similar to the one that had been displayed at my mother's wedding. Inside were two lovebirds, waiting to be presented to the bride and groom. Their job was to look pretty and coo happily while people passed and admired both their union and their charming house.

After an evening of eating, dancing, and making small talk with hundreds of friends and near strangers, Sandy and I, newlyweds, hopped in his shiny silver BMW and headed to the Grove Park Inn in Asheville, North Carolina. Within seconds of getting in the car, Sandy wadded up his rented tuxedo and threw it in the back seat, and I remember us laughing as we pulled out of the circular drive. It may not have been the head-over-heels kind of love, but we were young and I was excited by the idea of being bound and promised each to the other and exhilarated by the possibilities stretching before us.

But as we drove away from our family and friends, and it was only the two of us, I had another nagging thought that began to work its way up through the layers of giddy excitement. *Well, you've really gotten yourself in it now, Kreis. There's no getting out of this one.* Even at twenty-two, I had always had an escape plan, to the next-door neighbors', to my blue bedroom, to the pool at the country club, to college in New Orleans. This time, there was no exit strategy as Sandy and I cruised through the mountains at seventy miles per hour, toward what the minister had told us was supposed to be forever.

Chapter 4

AND BABY MAKES THREE

I'd never met anyone willing to spend as much on a meal as Sandy Beall. We started our honeymoon in Hilton Head, South Carolina, at Sandy's parents' house on Deer Island. It was a cute treehouse-style home on stilts to protect it from the tides. Our first night, Sandy found the finest restaurant in the area. It was a French place, La Maisonette, with a German chef named Boris, and the food was outstanding. I don't remember the exact meal but it was something like beef filet, oysters Rockefeller, Belgian endive and radicchio salad, scalloped potatoes, and an elegant molten chocolate cake, on a preset menu. What I remember more clearly was the cost. The bill came to more than a hundred dollars, which was a lot of money in 1975. I told Sandy it was delicious, but not something we could possibly do again. Sandy didn't say anything, but the next night, we got in the car and he drove us straight back to the restaurant where we had the exact same meal and spent even much more money on wine and extras. Our repeat appearance also made us friends with Boris and his wife. After the restaurant closed, we went to their house, opened another bottle of wine, and talked about restaurants. This might seem unusual for a honeymoon, but it was typical for Sandy Beall.

Sandy was no different the day after we got married than he had been the day before. There was no expectation that I would take care of him. He did not ask me to cook dinner, do the dishes, or go to the grocery store. If I wanted to, I did; if I didn't, it was no problem. We were like two friends who had signed a contract to live together, but when it came to meeting our own needs, he didn't ask me and I didn't ask him.

Sandy already owned a cute house, an original log cabin on Glenmary Road in Knoxville with a tiny contemporary addition. It had one bedroom, one bathroom, dining and living rooms, and a kitchen, but it was clearly a bachelor's house, with some ugly furniture and a very funky smell. Unfortunately for the house and for me, it was fully carpeted, even in the bathroom. The smell could be fixed by ripping out the carpet, but the furniture was more of a challenge. Mixed in with a brass bed and some pretty secondhand antiques were several major eyesores, particularly the sofa in a style that the 1970s called "early American," with a hard, upright wingback and a tufted skirt around the base. The skirt concealed a pair of rockers, and the whole thing was upholstered in a fabric decorated with red birds. At one point, when it was being moved in a pickup truck, a cushion had blown off. Sandy's mother had a new cushion made, but the only way to do it was by cutting a big piece of fabric off the back, patching the bare spot, and pushing the sofa against a wall. My mother came over and took one look at the Glenmary living room and said, "We are going shopping."

More than creating our shared home, however, work defined our early married life. Sandy has an endless capacity for work.

As a child, Sandy was already entrepreneurial, selling baby chicks at Easter. When he became an expert tennis player as a teenager, he would bring his practice partners and his friends to his room and try to sell them his tennis clothes or whatever else was in his dresser drawers.

By college, classes were a distant second to his entrepreneurial drive. He had a tennis scholarship to East Tennessee State, but was "burned out" on sports. His dad was a nuclear engineer but there were five children to put through school, so a scholarship was important. It was during the Vietnam War, and Sandy joined the Air National Guard at the University of Tennessee. He transferred to UT and prepared for training, until he broke his toe. The Guard reassigned Sandy to office duty and he started working at a Pizza Hut. He quickly became the manager and then the area director, all while he was still in college. For years, I gave him a hard time, saying that he probably never went to class, just to the pizza ovens and his director's desk.

The owner of the Pizza Hut franchisee territory in Knoxville really liked Sandy, and he was also dying of cancer. Before he passed away, he gave Sandy some stock and told him, "Sandy, the American dream is to have your own business, and you need to go into business for yourself." Sandy took that to heart. He sold the Pizza Hut stock, found some partners, and opened his first Ruby Tuesday in 1972. Concept restaurants were big in the 1970s. Sandy modeled Ruby Tuesday after PJ Clarke's, a legendary pub-style restaurant on the Upper East Side of Manhattan, decorated with Tiffany lamps and leather barstools. He wanted each restaurant to have an old-time feel, so he rented a truck, drove to New York's antique district, and stuffed it full of things to hang in the restaurant. When he got back, he hammered the nails and hung the décor on the walls himself.

The concept worked. By the time we were married, there were two Ruby Tuesdays in Knoxville, one in Chattanooga, one in Gatlinburg, and a fifth in Nashville. For years, he picked out things for his restaurants, until the number of locations got so big that he had to have people help him. When he opened a Ruby Tuesday in Memphis, he asked my mother to oversee the design.

I did not aspire to be a millionaire like Sandy did, but I was starting to think about my own career path. I had missed my internship with Howard Baker by getting married, although it certainly wasn't as if Howard Baker was waiting for me to come work for him. In 1975, the menu of professions for women was limited, primarily nurse, teacher, or lawyer. I thought law school would be the best fit. All fall, while Sandy continued to expand Ruby Tuesday, I worked as a paralegal, and we enjoyed being newlyweds. We went out to dinner, traveled on weekends, and had fun. Then sometime in January, I started throwing up.

After days of not feeling well, I called my gynecologist. At first he prescribed some antinausea pills, but after five days, those hadn't worked, so he told me to come but said there was no way I could be pregnant because I was on birth control. But, the pregnancy test came back positive. I represented the half percent failure-rate statistic. I sat in his office stunned. It wasn't that I didn't like children, or I didn't want children, but I had never even thought about them. A baby at twenty-three was not part of my admittedly vague life plans. My doctor told me to take it easy, and I thought petulantly, *No, I'm going to do whatever I want. If I want to take up jogging, I will.* I even wondered if I should consider an abortion, but I immediately realized there was no way I could do that. Not ever.

I didn't know what I was going to do with this baby, but like everything else in life, I decided that I would figure it out by myself. I certainly didn't call my mother and cry on her shoulder. She had been barely twenty-one when Keith was born—only in my mother's eighty-ninth year did I learn that she had been devastated when she found out that she was pregnant so young. After Keith was born, Mammy had swooped in and taken over. For years, Keith had been as much Mammy's child as my mom's and no one said anything about it.

I told Sandy that night, and he didn't have much to say except that we were going to need more space beyond our one-bedroom log cabin. That baby became the catalyst that started a chain of events in both our lives. It led us to search for a place and a life we could truly call home.

My sister, Keith, was already pregnant. Her son, Abby, was born three months before I was due. That summer, I would go over to Keith's and sit my swollen self on her couch and watch her with Abby. She'd ask if I wanted to hold him, and I'd shake my head and say, "Nope. I'm going to be doing that pretty soon. I'm just going to watch you." Subconsciously, I was hoping for some spark of motherliness to be made manifest in Keith so that I could absorb it, too. In the same way that my mother had watched New York models to become one, or I had watched my mother put together a room or an outfit to learn how to do the same myself, I was trying to observe my sister as a cheat sheet for my own motherhood. But Keith was as adrift as I was. We just didn't have the relationship or the words to admit it. We were still stuck at our childhood dinner table trying to navigate the Le Sueur peas.

Keith's one piece of practical advice was to hire a baby nurse: "Call Miss Freeman, here's her number." Miss Freeman's first question to me was "How long do you want me to stay?" Without missing a beat, I said, "Six months." She answered right back, "Oh no, you don't," so I asked how long she usually stayed. "Three to five days." I told her I would never know what to do in three to five days. We settled on two weeks of baby nursing.

I did one other thing to prepare. The Lamaze breathing method for natural labor was all the rage, so I signed Sandy and myself up for Lamaze classes. But Sandy was often traveling for Ruby Tuesday, and together we made only one class. I asked Sandy, "How do you think I'm going to do Lamaze if we've only been to one class?" His reply was "Just fake it." I answered, "I'm sure this will be one thing that I can't fake."

The early part of the pregnancy had been hard. I was very sick in the beginning and I was hospitalized once because of excess bleeding. I thought I had lost the baby, but it was a blood clot. When I was released, the doctor told me to take it easy. Instead, I started getting ready to move.

In the process of adding on to the log cabin, the contractor had found termites. Sandy's response was: time to get another house. We sold the cabin, which is still standing by the way, and bought a two-story brick house on Towanda Trail in Sequoyah Hills, the residential section of Knoxville where I had grown up. My mother and I drove to Atlanta to find furnishings for the house and nursery while Sandy stayed to handle the closing. When we got back two days later, Sandy had news. We weren't buying the Towanda Trail house—instead we were moving to another house, a larger, white Italian-style house on Lyons View, which, despite being near the river, did not have a river view.

Those two days were a preview of my real estate life with Sandy. We, or more specifically he, sold and bought houses at an astonishing speed. There were houses we bought that we sold within six months or even after a single summer. There was a family house that Sandy sold right out from under me. There were ugly houses that I never would have chosen that were bought as investments. There were vacation houses, town-houses, houses with separate guesthouses. He measured them by what he thought were a good location, "good bones," and a good view, but also by potential—what others had failed to see or were simply unwilling to do. Forty-some houses and I named them all, but today I need a written list to remember each one.

This time we were changing houses because one of Sandy's employees at the time had purchased Lyons View with money she embezzled from the Ruby Tuesday account. Sandy couldn't get the money back, so instead he took her house. But we couldn't move in for a few weeks, so in the meantime we would live in Sam and Mary Anne Beall's basement. I had no idea this would be the beginning of years of packing and unpacking. I assumed this was a temporary adventure, and simply said okay.

The Bealls' basement had a second kitchen, and late one af-ternoon I decided to fry some chicken on the stove. I left it splattering for a minute to run to the bathroom, and by the time I came back, there was a fire in the kitchen. We put the fire out, but we still had to call the fire department, and there was smoke damage to the walls. It didn't ruin the downstairs, but it made a big mess. All I could say to Mary Anne Beall was "I'm so glad this happened at your house instead of my parents'." And it was the truth. If it had happened in my parents' house, there would have been, as the old saying goes, "hell to pay." All Mary Anne and Sam were concerned about was my health.

Since my first forays to the Townsends' house next door on Kenesaw Street, I had known that other households operated differently from mine. But I thought of those differences as operational qualities: what was on the dinner menu, who had bath time when. I paid attention to how my best friend, Carolyn Post, had two different kinds of toothpaste in her bathroom, and when her dad would say, "Every day's Christmas," I assumed that referred to the pinball machines in their basement and the bowls of Hershey's candy kisses in the living room, not to how he doted on his two daughters and his wife. Communication, caring, and forgiveness inside a family were like a foreign language to me. I hardly understood them or recognized them, but I would start to learn them at Sam and Mary Anne Beall's home. During our whole married life in Knoxville, we could always find reasons and time to go to the Bealls' for dinner. At her table, Mary Anne would ask questions, and I knew she wanted to hear the actual answers. It was my first adult picture of true family, of a whole home, free of friction, where people could say anything, and it was what I wanted to re-create for Sandy's and my children.

If I wanted to create that family-centered life, I realized I needed to learn to cook. My mother was privately aghast that Sandy was the chief cook in our house, and likely thought that my "modern" view did not bode well for the future of my marriage. Of course, she would never say that, just as she would never say that she regretted not teaching me how to cook when I was young, beyond our evenings of cookies, fudge, and spaghetti and meatballs when my father was out of town. Instead, one winter morning, she called me up and invited me to go to a cooking class with her. She said she had signed up with a friend who had gotten sick and there was a spot to fill. Whether this was a ruse or true, I'll never know, but like walking into that Ruby Tuesday opening in Gatlinburg and shaking hands with Sandy Beall, this event I tagged along to would transform my life.

The class was held in the home of a woman named Kathleen Barron, who was a legend among Knoxville women. In about three hours, she showed us how to cook an entire gourmet meal featuring beef Wellington, Pont Neuf potatoes, and baked Alaska. Days before, I would have been proud of myself for frying an egg without blackening the sauté pan.

It was a revelation, although it is ironic that my favorite meal as a child was a hamburger and French fries, and the first dish I mastered was simply a high-end version of meat and potatoes. For months, I took every cooking class that Kathleen offered and made her recipes at home. In 1975, there were very few cookbooks, and most of those didn't have pictures in them. There was no Martha Stewart or Barefoot Contessa. It wasn't possible to scroll through Pinterest or to Google "dinner recipes." Cooking was just you, the food, and the kitchen. And I loved it. I loved the art of it, the simplicity of it, the way the individual ingredients came together to become a beautiful whole. Cooking was also something concrete that I could do from beginning to end in the course of one day. I didn't have to plan for tomorrow; what I got that morning could be put on the table that night.

My mother was right: cooking bonded me to Sandy. Another one of my early cooking instructors, Annemarie Huste, used to tell us, "To be a good cook, you have to really love to eat or have someone to cook for who really loves to eat." Sandy fell into the latter category, and he was also in the business. Food was both a passion and a livelihood. And it was where we built much of the foundation of our family.

During our first twelve months of marriage, I discovered the twin gravitational poles that would shape my life: the "look good" of my mother and the "feel good" of Mammy. In the beginning, the gorgeous surface perfection of my childhood, where everything was always fine, defined my wish to create a beautiful home. The nurturing side, the easy back-and-forth, Sunday dinner, pass-the-potatoes-and-hot-buttered-corn style of Mammy and the Bealls was something I also very much wanted, but it took me far longer to find. Indeed, so many times over the years, I thought I was creating the latter when really I was re-creating the former.

The heart may believe it knows what it wants, but in its deepest recesses, it wants what it knows.

Using a more beautiful script, I was simply recopying the pages from my past.

Not long after I found out I was pregnant, I quit my paralegal job. I had plenty of time to cook, so I started inviting friends over five nights a week to try out recipes. I quickly realized that it wasn't just food I loved—it was entertaining, too. I loved setting the table and even cleaning the dishes after everyone left. I would read a recipe, think it looked exciting, and go to the store. Once I had all the ingredients, I would start calling people to invite: old friends from high school, people Sandy knew from tennis or college. Most recipes were written to feed six or eight, and my guest list was set by the number of servings. But the most special part always occurred at the table. It made me happy to make other people happy with food. I called my dinners "a happy meal," and I wish I had trademarked that phrase before McDonald's did in 1979.

At the start, I had no grand dreams of making a career out of cooking and entertaining, or hosting and homes. In the mid-1970s, men were chefs, while women were cooks. We mostly did our cooking at home. Even one of my heroes, Julia Child, had backed her way into cooking. I often think of a scene from the movie *Julie and Julia,* where over dinner Julia Child, as played by Meryl Streep, tells her husband, Paul, that she doesn't know what she wants to do next. "I signed up for a hat-making class," she says.

"You like hats," Paul responds, adding, "What else do you like?" She thinks about it and then says, "Well, I like to eat." Julia Child, of course, did not go into the hat-making business; instead her "like" of eating and food would define the rest of her life and career. She also didn't sit around thinking about it—she just did it. I didn't sit around thinking, either. I just knew that I had found something I loved. Cooking and entertaining gave me a greater sense of joy and purpose than anything else I had in life thus far. At night, while Sandy read company reports, I fell asleep reading Craig Claiborne's recipes and menus.

Those small moments defined the way we approached our lives—we were doers, not people who sat around discussing, planning, and deliberating. We saw opportunity and reacted; we thought in concrete terms of how to bring a place or a specific idea to life. We had endless energy and were willing to take risks, or at least consider doing things that most people would never attempt in those years. Then, too, Sandy believed in constant change, and I believed in Sandy.

One evening, after our guests had left, Sandy looked at me over a stack of dishes and said, "Kreis, you know, if we are going to have people over every night, we might as well be in the inn business." I knew him well enough to realize he was serious.

So I said, "Great. Go find us one."

MANY WAYS
TO MAKE A BEAUTIFUL TABLE

———————◆———————

A table can be made out of anything—metal, wood, a fold-up card table with a cloth on top. What makes it beautiful is the giving: the more you give to it, the more you get out of it. Because a table is never simply a table: it is a universal sign of welcome. When my table comes together, there is the perfect moment when a guest walks in and thinks, Wow, she did this for me, because she wants me to be here.

The meal is the foundation of my table. For me, making a meal is a complete cycle of accomplishment, sped up. In several hours, I can start and finish the entire process, from shopping, to preparing, to setting the places, to cleaning. I like every part of it, all the hands-on busywork, from the cooking to putting out flowers and mixing colors, to using my silver and china, even if we are eating hamburgers or takeout. I enjoy cleaning up, too, putting on rubber gloves and doing the dishes alone, accompanied by loud music. But at its heart, a meal for the table is something I can collaborate on. The cooking, the setting of the table, the shopping, the cleanup—all of it can be shared. A meal at a table is also more than eating. It's a chance to gather family and friends, to ask everyone to pause, share stories, and share each other. Tables are where we create our traditions and our memories.

You can build your own table in whatever way suits you. It should reflect your style, whether that style is many bright colors or soft neutrals or something in between. If you think of your table as being like a canvas, you can change your linens, your dishes, your candles, and anything else depending on whether you want to be formal or informal. A tablecloth can elevate a meal of mac and cheese. If you love flowers, use them. If you don't, or don't have the budget or the time, a few votive candles can be a centerpiece—they are easy to clean—or a simple bowl of apples or oranges. Keep your centerpieces low so it is easy to have a conversation over them. You can use Grandma's china and crystal or put paper plates on a pretty tablecloth, indoor picnic–style. Set your table the day before to save yourself time. It is fine to mix and match chairs. I like having a pitcher of water and salt and pepper shakers and letting guests serve themselves—I often set out four different types of salt to add an easy, fun dimension.

Always have cake (as Julia Child said, "A party without cake is just a meeting"), although homemade ice cream sandwiches in summer are a close second. And remember, part of gathering around a table is being present with your guests, not pressuring yourself to create a photo-ready tablescape or so many perfect plates of food that by the time you sit down your own plate is cold.

When I have guests now, I tell everyone to sit next to someone they don't know or don't know well, to find a new connection. I also like to mix different types of people, kids, adults, people I know through business, people I know through church, single people, married, widows and widowers, different ages, really everyone. The whole circle of life can be shared at one meal.

If it's chilly, even if the only person sitting down is me, I will make a fire and sit at a small table. Whether I've had a good day or a bad day, I will feel grounded and at home.

One thing that has changed for me over the years is saying grace and actually meaning the words. Now each day, no matter how elaborate or how simple, saying grace before a meal reminds me that because we are able to gather together, we are able to nourish and sustain ourselves and those around us, we are able to give and to share. Our tables, whatever they are made of and however they are set, remind us to count our blessings.

Chapter 5

TWO NEWBORNS

My due date came and went, and what did Sandy and I do? We went to lunch at Bahu Container. It was a Saturday, and I was wearing an unflattering large red T-shirt with my pregnancy jeans, and my feet and ankles were so swollen that the only shoes I could fit into were a pair of Dr. Scholl's. About midway through my lentil soup, I felt something odd and said, "I think this is it." As usual, we had driven to the restaurant in two separate cars, Sandy having met me after coming from somewhere else. He nodded, got the check, and said, "I'll meet you at home. Get your suitcase and we'll go."

I pulled into the driveway of the Lyons View house, with its great sweeping yard where I loved cutting the grass on the riding mower, where Sam and Mary Anne Beall had brought over Lenten roses from their garden to plant, and where I had painted the nursery a truly ugly yellow so it would be the perfect color for either a boy or a girl. I shut off the engine, opened the door of my Volkswagen station wagon, and hauled myself out. I had taken maybe one or two steps before I felt a great wetness. I looked down, thinking my water had broken, but it was blood. I was standing in puddles of my own blood.

At that moment, Sandy pulled up. He took one look, told me to leave my shoes, helped me into his car, and we raced to the hospital. Seven minutes later at the ER door, I was lifted onto a gurney and rolled away. Someone checked the baby's heartbeat, and it was falling fast. The only option was an emergency C-section. I was given a quick spinal block, which, probably because I had just eaten, made me sick. The last thing I remember before giving birth was me throwing up lentils in the operating room as a team of panicked doctors and nurses stood over me.

Sam was born twenty minutes after we arrived at the hospital, less than thirty minutes after I had gotten out of my car.

I woke in the recovery room, opened my eyes, and saw the IV bags of blood and glucose hanging next to the bed. Machines were beeping and I had oxygen going into my nose and a tube down my throat. I couldn't talk, but I kept trying to get the nurse's attention across the room to ask, "What was it?" She finally looked at me and said in a chilly, crisp voice, "I can't understand you." I was scared and alone, and I didn't know if my baby was a girl or a boy, or if it was even alive.

For several days, I couldn't hold my baby and wasn't physically strong enough to even sit up. From the hemorrhage and the emergency C-section, I had lost nearly a third of my body's blood supply. Nothing in the glossy childbirth pamphlets with their smiling mothers and rosy babies had prepared me for this. No one popped a champagne cork and offered me a celebratory toast. Sam and I didn't snuggle up while he breastfed. Instead, he spent ten days in the hospital nursery while I tried to heal from the trauma. I was just grateful to be alive to meet him.

Baby Sam was absolutely beautiful. Like nearly all Caesarian children, he came out with a perfectly round head. I probably did thank God, but in a cursory, check-the-box kind of way. By the time I took Sam home, he had likely bonded more with the floor nurses than with me.

Sandy didn't stay at the hospital, but he had a catered lunch and dinner delivered to my room every day, his way of speaking love. My mother, who is a wonderful seamstress, made a white gown for Sam to go home in and a white lace cap with a blue trim, monogrammed with the letters SEB IV, for Samuel Erasmus Beall IV. Baby Sam was in fact the ninth Samuel Erasmus Beall, but Sandy's father had dropped his name back to Sam E Beall II so the numbers wouldn't go on and on. (Indeed, Sandy's given name is Samuel Erasmus Beall III.)

On the day we left the hospital, the nurse wheeled me to the curb, where Sandy was waiting with the car. I got in, and the second she handed me the baby—it was 1976 and no one used car seats—Sam started screaming. He cried the whole way home and didn't stop for a long time after that.

Sandy pulled into the driveway and honked the horn for Miss Freeman, the baby nurse. When she came out, he pushed the button to roll down the electric window, turned to me, and said, "I want to go out to lunch." After ten days in the hospital, I recoiled but said, "Sandy, I can't go out to lunch until I get my hair washed." He said, "That's okay. I'll sit with you." So we put Sam in Miss Freeman's arms, Sandy drove me to Kristopher's salon to have my hair washed, and then we went off to eat. Two days later, we left Sam again to escape for an overnight to Scona Lodge. Looking back now, I realize that I wasn't the only person in my marriage who always had an exit strategy.

Deep down, I was terrified. I believed that my body had almost killed this helpless baby. I knew nothing about being a mother and was certain the hospital nurses had been far better at soothing Sam. I convinced myself he was safer and better off at home with Miss Freeman. While I was pregnant, women around Knoxville would cluck that I would "just know what to do once the baby came." In my world, no new mothers were depressed or had watery stains on their blouses because milk had leaked out of their breasts, or needed more than the help of a good girdle to fit back into their old clothes. We all just effortlessly stepped into our updated role.

Except when some of us don't. For years, I have watched my granddaughters carry their baby dolls from room to room, seen how they carefully comb the dolls' hair, hold them, and take them for walks in the stroller. That was never me. I am fairly certain I didn't voluntarily pick up a baby doll at any point during my childhood. I didn't even babysit. At twenty-three, I was young, selfish, and completely unprepared. But I consoled myself that at least I had Miss Freeman.

Then, six days into her stay, she had to leave when one of her relatives died. After she left, I sat in the kitchen with Sam and we both cried. I would like to say that before long Sam and I adjusted, but we didn't—instead we just made a silent pact that we were going to get through this together. I strapped him to my chest and took him everywhere with me. We cooked together, we went to the grocery store. We even mowed the lawn together after I discovered that it was the only reliable way to get him to nap. He took after his mother in that regard; I am the world's worst napper.

I wasn't going to be anyone's choice for mother of the year, but like everything I had done up to that point, and everything I did after, I tried the very best I knew how. I wanted to love my children as they were, not wanting them to be thinner or faster, taller or funnier, or more serious or less serious. They could choose their sports, they could choose their lives. I would try to learn to adapt to them rather than the other way around.

At the same time Sam was born, Sandy and I adopted another child, a rundown six-bedroom inn named Blackberry Farm.

There are houses that strike you like a thunderclap, blocking out every other sound, their presence like an overwhelming vibration in the atmosphere. There are others that simply feel right from the moment you turn the key in the lock and step through the front door. And then there are those houses that are not quite right, where things have been neglected and there is a sense that something is off, rooms set in the wrong way or bisected by unnecessary walls, floor joists showing their age, stairs with an awkward turn, windows mismatched, yet you find yourself drawn through them, deeper and deeper, until you have dead-ended in a small back closet. It is as if the house has worked its way under your skin, the plain girl whose face is transformed when she smiles. That was Blackberry.

I did not think, *I have to have this house.* The location was awkward, at the end of West Millers Cove, a narrow road of peaks, valleys, and curves, about twenty feet wide. Where the asphalt dead-ended, we turned left into a gravel drive. I knew we were sitting on a rise in the land, but trees and scrubby brush obscured the wider view. I could only suppose what might lie on the other side. The house was not imposing, a one-and-a-half-story with dormers on the front and back, built from a combination of fieldstones and white shake shingles, with a slate roof. It had been constructed in the 1930s and was now on its second owner. Inside, most of the doors were closed, except for the warm kitchen, which had two big chairs in it and looked like it hadn't been touched since the 1940s. The living room had wooden floors and a big bay window. It was decorated with buckets of artificial flowers and, for unknown reasons, a water pump. Even the name was unassuming—the farm had been christened when the first owner snagged her silk stocking on a blackberry bramble.

Yet there was something about this unassuming place, something that made me want to walk through the rooms again, to breathe in the warmth of the kitchen, to sit in a rocker on the back stone porch and listen to the wind rustle the early spring leaves. It seemed as if it were waiting expectantly for its own Cinderella story to unfold or simply waiting for a young couple who foolishly thought, *Sure, we can run an inn* to come along.

Make no mistake, we were foolish. I was four or five months pregnant, hardly the time to become an innkeeper. But the way some men love cars or football, Sandy loves acquisition. He was intrigued about the idea of us running an inn, so he began looking and asking around for properties to buy. One person he called was Lamar Alexander. Sandy had worked on Lamar's unsuccessful run for Tennessee governor in 1974. But even more important for us, Lamar was from Maryville, the cute town between Knoxville and the Smoky Mountains. Lamar said, "I know a place."

I never asked Sandy where we were going to get the money to buy Blackberry, let alone fix it up, and we never sat down to discuss the pros and cons. I had complete faith and left the finances to him. I just wanted to cook and have people over. Sandy financed the purchase using two banks. He sent a photographer to take pictures of my parents' vacation house in

North Carolina. He showed the "before" photographs of Blackberry and the "after" of my mother's decorating to the loan officers, with a promise, "This is what it will look like when we get finished with it."

He—and my mother's design—must have been incredibly persuasive, because not only did they agree to finance the purchase, but he negotiated a deal with the Bank of Maryville to lease Blackberry Farm for its own weeknight business entertaining. He did the same thing with our other lender in Nashville, allowing them to use Blackberry as an employee perk and weekend retreat. The lease payments we received from those two banks covered our mortgage bill.

The first person I called once our bid was accepted was my mom. I told her we were opening an inn and asked if she would decorate it. My mother was just like me, she asked no questions, she simply said "Sure," and she did. She went shopping, saw what fabric was on the bolt, what could work in our budget, and then she set about matching colors and pieces to make it look like a full-on English country house in the foothills of the Great Smoky Mountains. When she showed me the five different fabrics that she was planning to put in the living room, I thought it would all clash and be too much, never having bothered to notice that she had done the exact same thing in designing her own beautiful living room. Sandy and I moved our furniture into the house, and we brought our wedding china, crystal, and silver, which was plentiful thanks to the eight hundred guests. But we still needed basic furnishings like beds, tables, and chairs.

Mom, Sandy, and I went to auctions almost every weekend and I scoured friends' attics and basements for cast-off pieces. After watching my mother, I learned what to pick and how to arrange it. We redid the bedrooms and the rest of the house, painted, wallpapered, built a tennis court, and fixed the pool, the first of my "engagement rings."

When the renovations were completed, Sandy, I, and four-month old baby Sam moved full-time to Blackberry Farm—Blackberry and Sam "arrived" so close together, they were practically twins. I put baby Sam in the room I had named Holly, with a beautiful view of the Smoky Mountains. Sandy and I were in a back room, to which I gave the very basic name Brown French, because its walls were covered in a brown and white toile. Any guests who stayed overnight were a doorway or two away in our tiny upstairs hall.

I went about learning how to be an innkeeper, which I decided was basically repeating what I had done at home, cooking and entertaining. If I felt stuck, I tried to channel the influence of my mother and my grandmother. I knew that I wanted my home to look like Mom's and to feel and taste like Mammy's. My mother's beautiful physical design would attract customers, while Mammy's love of a welcoming table and making others happy would make them want to stay and return. Those two philosophies became the driving force at Blackberry. The rest I made up as I went along.

Chapter 6

FAMILY BUSINESS

Some weeks, I wasn't sure if I was married to Sandy Beall or to Blackberry first.

I had always learned best by doing, and at Blackberry, I did pretty much everything. We had to at least break even financially and Sandy had a real job. He used to say, "If we make two hundred decisions a day and hit eighty percent, we are doing good." And that's exactly what it felt like. There was hardly any time to think before or after a decision.

I planned the evening's menus based on what I had learned in cooking school or found in a cookbook, sometimes fillet with Bordelaise sauce or Queen Elizabeth chicken, and chocolate mousse or reine de saba for dessert. French cooking was considered the height of good cuisine. There was no commercial food delivery for a small business like ours, and even if there had been, we would have had nowhere to store it.

With Sam in tow, at least three times a week I drove thirty minutes each way to Maryville to shop at Kroger, the only place for food. The concepts of "farm to table" or "locally sourced" didn't exist back then around Knoxville, or really anywhere other than some tiny slivers of California.

I spent upwards of six hours each day planning and cooking. On Saturdays, we served three meals a day, starting with a country breakfast featuring pancakes, eggs, and grits, and like every other meal, it came out of the kitchen on our wedding china. The rest of the time, I set the tables, arranged the flowers, cleaned the pool, and when the grass got too tall, I mowed it, with Sam sitting on my lap. I'd hold him with one arm and steer the riding mower with the other.

It quickly became clear that Sandy and I needed help. We hired a young married local girl, Wendy, to assist with the housekeeping, and an ex–army cook named John to join me in the kitchen. John was tall and skinny, a hippie with a ponytail. He showed up for his interview wearing a blue polyester leisure suit that he had borrowed. I liked him immediately, and he ended up working with us at Blackberry for fifteen years.

Sam loved to be in the kitchen every bit as much as I did. I would set him in a playpen next to me, and he played with pots and pans while I baked fresh bread and squeezed oranges to make juice that we left on little trays outside each door at dawn for our overnight guests. When he started walking, I let him carry out the bread basket on a tray. He would toddle forward in his red footie pajamas or fluffy blue sleeping suit, like a bunny without the ears, and it was the cutest darn thing anyone had ever seen. He was in constant motion, never sitting down long enough to eat a meal, so I stuck his plate on a low shelf where his toddler arms could reach. He would stand up and take bites of his main foods, Cheerios and quiche, when his time permitted. He hated missing any part of the action.

Most weeknights, Sandy walked into the kitchen around seven to find John behind the industrial stove, Sam in his playpen or squirming in his highchair, and me getting the plates ready to serve. John would finish plating dinner and Sandy and I would serve our guests. If the food didn't turn out perfectly, we had our few quick fixes; an extra dollop of butter or a sprinkle of salt and guests didn't notice. Thankfully for us, there wasn't much of a food culture during those years. If any of our guests were difficult, we just, in Sandy's words, "poured a glass of wine and got through it." After the plates were cleared and Sam was asleep, the three of us would reconvene in the kitchen to set up for breakfast. For Sunday brunch, Sandy and I would poach eight eggs each while John made the hollandaise sauce. Our routine never deviated: we were a perfectly tuned trio, with a rhythm that I truly loved.

In the kitchen, I evolved to having preset menus so that whoever was coming made their choices before they arrived. The car dealers and the Bank of Maryville bankers came to play poker and smoke cigars, and they expected prime rib with stuffed potatoes and chocolate pie. On weekends, we offered two different entrées, either chicken or beef, usually prime rib. Fortunately, I didn't have to worry about alcohol and mixing drinks. My brief stint in college as a cocktail waitress had proven that I had no business behind the bar—I used to divide the drinks on my tray into groups of brown or white and then I would ask each patron to point to his or her glass. But at Blackberry I was off the hook. Blount County was a dry county, so guests brought their own liquor and poured their own cocktails.

My last hire was a nanny/housekeeper, Elma, a country woman from Cocke County, the roughest county in Tennessee, who had what I believed were coffee stains on her teeth, but were actually from a wad of chewing tobacco. I was working nonstop and needed a nanny because I was pregnant again.

Before Sam had turned one, I had decided it was time for another baby because I thought he should have a playmate, but I didn't plan on getting pregnant and having another baby so quickly. Seventeen months after Sam burst into the world in a pool of blood, his brother, David, was born with almost no drama via a scheduled C-section. Sam had been named after his father, and David was named after my father. I didn't consider any alternatives. That was simply how things were done in my family and so many others, an easy running stitch of first and last names repeated across the generations.

This second time around, everything was easy: the pregnancy, the delivery—a scheduled birth was perfect for Sandy's hectic business schedule—even having a newborn. When it came time to leave the hospital, Sandy wasn't in town to drive us home, but that didn't strike me as unusual. Instead my mom took us in my dad's Cadillac.

Mom and I nestled David on a pillow wedged between us in the front seat. He slept the entire way to Blackberry, my mother stealing glances at his still little body while she gripped the wheel. David slept like that almost anytime, anywhere. Where Sam had been a colicky baby who calmed down only when he was asleep on the riding mower or strapped to my chest in the baby carrier, David was a sweet, floppy baby who just wanted to be held. I carried him around while I worked in the kitchen. He would drape himself over the bend in my arm, hanging like a wet spaghetti noodle. Everyone in the family took to calling him Noodle and we passed him among our outstretched arms.

He started walking late, and I always thought it was because we held him too much.

With David's arrival, we needed another bedroom. Sandy and I shifted into a room called Magnolia, Sam moved in to Blue French, which had blue toile on its walls, and I put David's crib in a room that was more like a large walk-in closet with a window.

I had no idea how lucky I was. We were living right in the middle of the upstairs, with guests on either side. I cannot imagine if David had been a fussy baby and not a perfect angel. What if visitors had spent good money to be kept up by a crying infant? Perhaps God knew that one fussy baby was probably all I could handle.

There's an old country saying that if you lift the calf from the time it's born, you can lift the cow when it's grown, meaning that you grow with the challenges. In those first years of marriage and parenthood, Sandy and I had merged business, family, strangers, and friends. Everyone sat at our table, and entertaining and having people over became like breathing.

But when Sam turned three, I felt in my gut that it was time to move. The logistics of raising two small boys in an out-of-the-way inn were hard. There were no neighborhood games, no friends' houses, no playroom at Blackberry, no preschool. It was time to come down from the mountain.

Sandy brought in Gary Doyle, a Ruby Tuesday manager, to run Blackberry day to day. Gary and his wife, Bernadette, became our super husband-and-wife team throughout the 1980s. Bernadette replaced me in the kitchen. She did everything I did, except that she did it longer and better.

Sandy and I packed up what few personal items we had and

moved back to Knoxville. Our new place on East Hillvale Road was a small three-bedroom, two-floor duplex built in the 1940s. I thought we would be there forever, or at least until the boys were out of elementary school. I think we stayed about six months. This was the start of our first stretch of nomadic years, where we packed and unpacked boxes and the moving van came and went with regularity. I learned to take Polaroid photos of the contents of each box, tape it to the outside, and to mark the room where it belonged, so I could unpack fast.

But in all those years that we moved houses, leaving behind a trail of addresses and endlessly forwarded mail, it felt like we never truly moved homes. Something in both of us held on to Blackberry. I don't know if it would have been easy to sell, but it didn't matter because we never considered it. Knowing that our children and someday grandchildren and great-grandchildren could run around and have a place to call home was what made me so protective of Blackberry.

For Sandy, it was also about family, having a place to share with others, and a pure love of the land. His father was from Lumpkin, Georgia, where the Beall family had a 730-acre farm, or as they called it, a plantation that grew cotton, corn, and peanuts. As a child, Sandy's dad, Sam Beall, learned to drive the family's Ford out the rough, rutted back roads so that his father could take a measure of the crops as they traveled. There was something about rural land baked into both Sandy and me, something that kept Blackberry as our place of permanence, the one home we would never give up, the place where we knew we would always return.

Ruby Tuesday was a large part of the reason why we began moving. Sandy was opening restaurants in multiple states and traveling constantly. In 1982, he sold the company to a restaurant conglomerate and at ages twenty-nine and thirty-two, we became paper millionaires.

But part of the reason was also us. Many Southern men of his era love game and bird hunting, Sandy, however, loves the hunt for a house. In a little more than three years, we moved to three different houses in Knoxville. Then, almost on a whim, we decamped for Hilton Head, South Carolina. Sandy was going to be gone four nights a week as part of his work for Morrisons, the company that was absorbing Ruby Tuesday. He could fly in and out from anywhere, so we reasoned why not a place with a beach, a bay, and an ocean? Sandy had never lived outside of Knoxville; my only time away had been during college. So why not an adventure?

Chapter 7

KEITH

While it is natural for us to assume that we are the authors of our own lives, the ones to oversee our own grand plans, looking back now I think we relocated to Hilton Head not for us, but for my sister. It was not our lives that God was most worried about during those years, but Keith's life and those of her children. She was the one who had to leave Knoxville. Sandy and I simply had to go first. Since she was ten years old, Keith had built her entire life around horses. Her closest friends were her fellow equestrians. She would drive out to the stables with four other girls in a big, beat-up white Oldsmobile that they nicknamed White Trash. The adults planning the rest of Keith's life didn't seem to realize how central horses were to her identity, and even Keith didn't fully appreciate it herself. At the Webb School, the headmistress recommended she apply to Centenary College for Women, a junior college in Hacketts-town, New Jersey. It had an equestrian center, but Dad thought it was too expensive for Keith to bring her horse, and in college, she didn't ride. Instead of the glistening brown coat and comforting nuzzle of her filly, food became her most reliable friend. She gained sixty pounds in twenty-four months. As she says now, "In those two years, my train went off its tracks."

Back in Knoxville, it wasn't long before she got into drugs and alcohol. The drugs made her thin, and she began dating a man named Jack Carter. Jack was a charismatic, charming con artist. They eloped in 1974, getting married in neighboring Maryville. Mammy bought them a tiny, cute house on Holloway Drive; the payments were $127 a month. She gave Keith the keys, saying that she did not want her "to ever have to ask *that man* for one thing." That man was not Jack—it was our father. But while Mammy could try to shelter Keith from our father, Mammy couldn't protect my sister from her own poor choices in men, just as no one had been able to protect Mammy. When she got married in 1927, Mammy was given two large diamond rings that had been in her family. During one of his benders, Pappy took one ring and sold it for cash. Decades later, the second ring was stolen and sold by Keith's drug dealer husband.

Jack didn't just deal drugs, he used them, and Keith and Jack tried whatever he sold: pot, cocaine, heroin. The only time she didn't use drugs was when she was pregnant. I knew none of this until years later, and I had no idea how bad things were until Keith called me and said that Jack had knocked her teeth out. She was rushing to the dentist and needed me to watch her two boys, Abby and Dylan, who were almost the same ages as Sam and David. Babies were about the only thing we had in common, the only point where our lives intersected.

Not long after the teeth incident, I tried to find my way into a relationship with my sister. We began by Keith and me going shopping. We left our shopping bags in her car, and Jack, who always kept tabs on everything that Keith did, stole them out of the car. When we discovered they were gone, Keith's first words were "Jack took them." I was shocked. I said, "You've got to be kidding. What would he do with all that?" Keith answered, very matter-of-factly, "Sell it." I called Jack and told him, "We want the shopping bags back." He hung up on me, so I kept calling. The calls and hang-ups continued until I got out the word "Now." He said, "I don't have them," to which I replied, "Oh yes, you do." And then he said, "You can't prove it." By this time, Jack was on court-ordered probation. "Who do you think your probation officer will believe?" I shot back, adding, "I'll tell him I saw you do it." Every bag reappeared in the trunk that afternoon. Keith was stunned, both that I had stood up to him and that it had worked.

When Dad realized how much danger Keith was in, he orchestrated several interventions, including one at a Shoney's out in West Knoxville, with the six of us—Mom, Dad, Sandy, me, and Keith and Jack. Keith tried rehab, but the only chance to save her was to get her away from her husband.

After I moved to Hilton Head, Keith's friend Mellie and I came up with a plan. One of the few things Jack would allow Keith to do was to take the boys to swim at the country club with Mellie. I told her, "Pick up Keith, Abby, and Dylan, go swimming, and when you get back in the car, don't go home, just drive straight to Hilton Head." Mellie, true to her word, did just that. Without so much as a change of clothes, she drove them directly to our gated community. The boys arrived still wearing their little swimsuits, now dry and stiff from the chlorine. Once that gate closed behind them, Keith never went back.

Jack moved to Washington State, where he took up with a

new girlfriend. One night when they were both high, Jack beat her head against the wall, killing her. That poor woman could have so easily been Keith.

Keith, Abby, and Dylan lived with us until she found a house to rent, and her boys lived with us on and off for years. It was a foursome of Sam and Abby and David and Dylan, who caught their first fish together off the dock in Hilton Head when I left them out with baited hooks, never thinking they would catch anything, only to have them reel in a fish almost big enough for supper. It was the four boys who would eat my homemade grape juice popsicles and have the purple juice run sticky around their cherry-red mouths and drip down in little streams and tributaries along their rounded stomachs. I can still picture them in their cute little Speedo-style bathing suits. It was the four boys who learned to ride bikes and build sandcastles and shower outside to at least rinse off the first layer of sand.

Keith and I also could not have done it without Sandy. Always supportive, he never complained. He became the first male figure in Keith's life who reliably stuck up for her. Ironically, they even shared shoes. Sandy and Keith wore the same size running shoes, and she borrowed his sneakers and sometimes even his cowboy boots. To Sandy, we were all family, Keith was welcome, and that was that.

Our families were also interwoven in other, less dramatic ways. Sandy's brother, Price, was going to open a restaurant in Hilton Head, and I signed on as a partner. We named it Truffles.

My vision was to model it after the café restaurants with adjoining prepared food markets, like Dean and DeLuca, which were popping up around New York City. We planned to open over Fourth of July weekend, at the height of the summer season, and we were desperate for staff. Keith was my bread baker. I hired a Knoxville girl to come stay with us and watch the boys. Together, Keith and I would rise at five-thirty a.m. and go to Truffles. We had our routine; take out the loaves of frozen bread that came from Vie de France, prep, and finish them in the kitchen proofing ovens so they were piping hot, bagged, and ready for sale. We also made pastries for the breakfast rush. Lunch had its own rhythm. We had three line cooks at the restaurant, I usually worked behind the line, Price ran the restaurant floor, and Keith ran the market.

The whole time Keith was drinking. She hid it well and never missed a morning. I spent more than two years in Hilton Head with her, and until the end, I didn't have any idea how much liquor she was consuming. Only when she had her own place and I talked to her on the phone late at night could I hear the clink of her glass, the ice hitting the side, or the slightly too hard way that she would set it back down. Then I knew. Today, she will tell you anything about how much she drank and how she would black out. One time, she wrecked her car with Abby sitting loose in the back seat. As Keith says, every alcoholic promises "Today will be the day," but for years, it never was.

Finally, she did call me, and said, "Kreis, this time I'm going to do it. I'm checking myself into a thirty-day program." But while it's possible to stop drinking in thirty days, it doesn't change your life. You have to learn how to manage every single day.

I remember our whole family, including Mom and Dad, going to meet with her rehab doctor, Dr. John. One thing he said stuck with me: that when Keith got cleaned up and away from all drinking and all drugs, she would be at the same emotional maturity level as when she began her addictions. If she started drinking and doing drugs at eighteen, she would return to the sober world with the maturity of an eighteen-year-old. I don't know if that is technically true, but sometimes I think it applies to me just as much as to Keith. I became addicted to work when I was twenty-three, and when I woke up, I had the emotional maturity of around a twenty-three-year-old. And I think the same was true for Sandy.

A GOOD-ENOUGH HOST

Some of the people least likely to be invited for dinner are good home cooks and professional chefs. Their friends and family are intimidated; they believe they cannot measure up. There was a time when I felt that way, felt that my best presentation always had to be on display. But in this season of my life, I realize that what matters is to be a good-enough host.

A good-enough host is fine with serving takeout on platters or straight from the containers, or eating sitting on stools at the kitchen island. A good-enough host is authentic to who they are and what they have to offer, whether it is pizza, burgers, or a full sit-down dinner. A good-enough host cares most about the gathering, about being warm, honest, fun, and welcoming.

In the age of Instagram, we can be so focused on taking a photo of the perfect place setting or the perfect dish that we can forget to record the true memory. Good-enough is about slowing down to appreciate the good, to make sure that everyone has a place in the conversation, that we go around the table to answer a question. That we make meaning by being. A good-enough host is good enough to sit at her or his own table and not spend most of the meal racing in and out of the kitchen.

One of my favorite books (and favorite concepts) is Radical Hospitality *by Lonni Collins Pratt. It says that the answer to modern-day distrust and fear is hospitality. Radical hospitality is the opening of our hearts to another; it is listening, and giving what you have. If all you have is canned soup, but you serve it with love and are interested in your guest, then that is good enough. That is hospitality.*

You can offer radical hospitality to total strangers, to friends, and to family. It is the hospitality of being known and wanting to be known. Today, I practice radical hospitality with my grandchildren. At Monday-night dinners, my table is as much a home for Barbies, crayons, games, and art projects as it is for food. Their favorite activities are waiting for them. I remember and rotate their dinners: Rose's adored chicken parmesan, Sam's beef, crunchy Brussels sprouts for Josephine, and a plate of little appetizers for Lila, who loves to walk around and pass hors d'oeuvres. If my mother is with us, or Sandy's father, Sam, I make sure they have the best vantage point, to see it all and soak it in, because that is what they love. Truth be told, that is what I love as well.

Chapter 8

HILTON HEAD

Creating a restaurant in Hilton Head was not as crazy as it sounded. I already had experience with commercial food preparation, not only at Blackberry but when we lived in Knoxville. I knew how to cook and how to sell, and I was comfortable with restaurant concepts and commercial kitchens. For several years, I worked for my first cooking teacher, Kathleen Barron, who had a catering service. I cooked for her in my kitchen and then drove the food to her house.

It was vintage early-1980s elegant food, Silver Palate–style. I'd poach whole salmons and arrange platters of cold marinated chicken with savory vegetables. I made country pâtés and cucumber soup. I would prepare two hundred box lunches for the arts festival or a wedding and think nothing of it. When Sam and David wanted to play, I gave them vegetables, cutting boards, and knives and taught them the basics of chopping. Once a friend walked in and was horrified that I was letting my boys use sharp blades, but I kept them right on chopping.

Sandy had also put me in charge of revamping a former Ruby Tuesday test kitchen in Knoxville that was being turned into a restaurant called Fitzgerald's. His instructions were "I want you to make it sing." Sandy supplied me with someone who knew how to manage the business end; my responsibilities were the concept and the quality. I decided to fashion Fitzgerald's into a crêperie after one I had seen in Atlanta. By the time I got to Hilton Head, we had the perfect arrangement: I got to work on developing the initial vision, Price managed the operations, and Sandy was the financial backer.

Before Truffles opened, I took Sandy and Price to New York. Previously, when I had visited New York, my friends couldn't pull me out of the gourmet shops. The stores and their gorgeous, overflowing platters of prepared food were all the rage in Manhattan, but much of the South didn't have anything like it. I had never seen platters of bright green beans, blanched and dressed with oils and sesame seeds, crunchy broccoli, whole cloves of garlic, and green salads of every description. At home, our "salads" were anything bound with mayonnaise, like potato salad, coleslaw, or chicken salad. The only lettuce I could buy was iceberg, and a "lettuce salad" was iceberg topped with canned pineapple, mayo, and grated cheese.

Sandy, Price, and I ate our way from Zabar's to Dean and DeLuca, Silver Palate, and other gourmet shops, with me saying, "I want to try something like this" at Truffles. I imagined cases laden with beautiful fresh food so locals and customers on vacation could choose the perfect dinner. Together, we settled on the concept of opening a sit-down restaurant with a take-out food shop and a bakery, because I loved to bake. We made Truffles a Vie de France franchise—a high-end bakery company—and Price and I spent a week training at their headquarters, learning how to thaw baguette dough, put it in rollers, score it, and proof it in the proof box. We offered four different types of croissants and fresh-squeezed orange juice, which I insisted had to be done by hand and not with a press, because a press gets oils from the peel and rind into the juice—Keith still remembers, not fondly, squeezing the juice. We sold jams and dressings from the Silver Palate. We had a constant stream of people who rotated in and out of Hilton Head to work at Truffles and live with us, so much so that when Keith and I left before five-thirty in the morning, more than likely we would be playing musical cars, moving parked vehicles around so we could get our own cars out of the driveway.

I enjoyed the rhythm of restaurant work. It reminded me of swimming: the consistency and repetition of the tasks, the pushing through to the next lap. And for someone who never enjoyed team sports, I liked something else about it. I made my own decisions, did things my own way, and in my own time.

In a vacation paradise, Sandy and I were living a vacation marriage. He was gone all week on business and home on the weekends, when we would go to the beach or out in a boat. He deferred all the decisions at home to me because he was so rarely there—except for the decisions on where we would live.

Typical Sandy and Kreis, we stayed in Hilton Head for a little over three years, and in that time we lived in four different homes, opened two businesses, and went on more boat trips than I can remember. Without thinking, we developed a parallel play–style relationship, moving side by side, the way toddlers start out playing, each pushing their own push toy, chasing their own ball, or stacking their own set of blocks.

I was never bothered by our time apart or the fact that I saw Sandy only on weekends. To me, we were just as effective together or apart. We fit together the way a well-loved baseball glove knows its owner's hand.

On the days when Sandy was gone, we talked on the phone. When he was home, we loved being with each other probably more than any other couple we knew. We were in sync, down to how we dressed. Years later, Sam and his wife, Mary Celeste, went to a Halloween party dressed as Sandy and me, in our complementary tailored, preppy uniforms—mine being blue jeans and a tucked-in Oxford shirt with the sleeves rolled up, a belt, white Keds, and a string of pearls, Sandy wearing a similar Oxford shirt, jeans, and tasseled loafers without socks, and carrying a roll of architectural plans. At first I didn't get the joke, neither of us had noticed how easily we had become each other's doppelgänger.

The only time I can remember being really irritated with Sandy was when he brought some Ruby Tuesday executives to see Truffles. One of them asked a question, and as I was answering, Sandy jumped in and took over the response. I was upset at being shut down: to me, it felt like another mother was answering a question about my child. I knew almost nothing about what went on in his business, but the opposite was also true: he knew very little about Truffles's day-to-day operations. But that was about the extent of any conflict.

---

*When two people are successful,
it is easy to gloss over any problems
and just keep going and doing.*

Hilton Head was a great place to live because no one was from there. We were all young professionals following our careers. It was natural to make friends with our interior designer, which we did, or with people in law, business, restaurants, and real estate, Sandy's passion. On weekends, Sandy scoured real estate listings to spot a good deal. After he had found four things he liked, we would jump in the car and go see them. Sandy could talk about every piece of property for sale.

Hilton Head is a barrier island with two sides, the ocean side and the bay, or what they call the cay-facing side. The cay is the sunset side, the calmer, smoother water side, and I liked the water and the sunset. I did not want to look across and see a big expanse of ocean. I wanted to see land on the other side of my water. I prefer valleys and the middle distance, because I like seeing borders and feeling the coziness of boundaries, which comes from being confined. After three houses, including a classic beach house that sat on pilings and shook in the smallest storm to the point where I had nightmares about the house vibrating around me, I found *my* dream house on the Calibogue Cay, with eggplant lacquered floors, a little lighthouse tower, and a wall of windows that faced the water and those perfect sunsets. Sandy made it happen by negotiating a trade, and we packed up and moved again.

In all this trading of places and locations, I never thought about the dreams of my popsicle-stained children, about whether they liked our house that was colored like an Easter egg or the oddly shaped one that I named the Dog House, where the deer got stuck in the aboveground pool, or our shaky beach house, or this one on the Cay.

When Sam was in kindergarten, he was playing with his friend Archer Crose while I was at work. Suddenly, Archer's mother, Mary Hunter, was on the phone to say that Sam was missing. I raced over and we began to search. An hour later, we found Sam at home. He had gotten ticked at Archer and had quietly left on his bike. The Croses' house and ours were less than ten minutes apart, but the only way Sam knew to find his way home was to ride all the way to our old house and then make his way to our current one. It was hard to know which house was home.

It is fitting that in a family that avoided communication, where it was possible to move houses without so much as a discussion, both of our children ended up with speech issues. It was probably also genetics. Sandy simply hadn't talked as a young child, while Sam and David were both born with some type of speech impediment. Sam stuttered into adulthood. David talked, but he had a language all his own. He ran his words and sentences together into one long, incongruous sound. Other children had no problem understanding him—Sam became his brother's translator—but adults, myself included, were often mystified. So many times, David would say something and I would turn to Sam with a confused look on my face and ask, "What did your brother just say?"

Those early speech patterns defined us more than we could know—Sandy's reticence in initiating discussions or having more intimate conversations, Sam's quiet dominance, David's maneuverability, his ability to tack in any direction depending on the prevailing currents and the wind, and my own inability to ask more than a superficial question, instead just trying to read between the lines.

One of my first conclusions was that Sam was born old. From the time he could stand up, he was determined, as much as any adult, to be in charge. On his first day of kindergarten, he started to board his bus only to pause on the steps, point at the driver, and say, "Mom, are you sure this guy knows where to take me?" In class, he wasn't particularly interested in learning his ABCs, but he liked to walk around the room and check everyone else's work. He also took it upon himself to line the kids up to walk to the cafeteria, and he made sure the teams were fair on the playground.

Given my own history with Keith, there was something strikingly naïve in my conviction that David would automatically become a playmate for Sam. They did play, with Sam directing the action, but having such a strong older brother meant David had to define himself by cultivating an unconventional streak. When David was about four—the age when Sam had been obsessed with the Incredible Hulk—he was fascinated by the grocery bag boys at the White Store. They were dressed in a signature uniform of gray pants, a white shirt, and a red bow tie—the same one they had worn since I was a child. All David wanted was to look like those bag boys, so while other mothers bought play clothes from Carter's and Garanimals, I dressed my younger son in gray pants, a white shirt, and a red bow tie and he loved it.

So much of our life revolved around restaurants, it shouldn't have come as a surprise that David was supremely adventurous with food and would eat anything. He tried foie gras when he was six, caviar and oysters before he turned ten. When Keith took him on a Disney Big Red Boat cruise, he told an adult couple seated at their table to pass on the steak and try the salmon with escargot because it was "quite nice." Even his pets were different. He never wanted a dog—birds were his passion, so over the years, we accumulated a small aviary, including a parakeet, as well as a trained talking yellow-naped parrot that he christened Baby after the character in *Dirty Dancing,* and later a duck that toddled around inside the fence in my vegetable garden.

My friend and decorator Kitty Cook was the person who told me we needed to have our family portrait painted, which was very much a thing on Hilton Head. Sandy and I selected an artist named Marge Parker, but we never discussed size, composition, or color. When the portrait was finished, it was enormous. The people were in clear focus, but everything else slightly abstract, and all of it done in soft, creamy colors.

We hung it, and Sandy gave it a nickname, "Mom and Her Three Boys," because he looked so young and boyish. He told me to ask Marge to "fix" him so he looked older. She said all she could do was add some shadows to his face—he really did look that young. But years later what struck me about the image that Marge had captured in those oils was that there were four individuals in that picture, primarily held together by the boundary of the canvas. Sandy, David, and I are looking off to the right, while Sam looks left. Aside from the common colors, it almost appeared as if we were occupying four separate portraits.

We moved that painting from house to house, admiring it, passing by it, but it was a long time before I truly looked at it and saw what it revealed.

I have one other memory from that period that stands out in stark relief. A year or so after we arrived in Hilton Head, I was working at Truffles and lost track of time. I had to pick Sam up at school, and when I glanced at my watch, I realized I had completely forgotten about my child. The entire way, I gunned the engine, berating myself.

When I pulled up, I expected a teacher or administrator to be waiting with a stern look. But there was no one. I started walking to the door, and suddenly there was a small rustling in the bushes. I turned and saw two blue eyes staring at me. The branches parted and seven-year-old Sam emerged. He had been hiding since dismissal, when he realized that my car was nowhere in the pickup line. Sam got in the back seat without a word as I began sputtering apologies and trying to comfort him by promising never to let it happen again. He didn't speak to me the entire ride, just stared out the window. When we got home, he marched straight to his room.

Eventually he came downstairs to ride his bike and play with his brother. I should have taken stock in that moment, perhaps said something to him, but instead I merely vowed to myself to do better.

In truth, I changed absolutely nothing. Work consumed me. I believed I was working on behalf of my family, it didn't feel selfish to me, so I did not slow down. I did not become a better listener. I did not wander out on the dock with my boys and drop a fishing line or a crab trap. I did not leave the dishes in the sink so I could go roast marshmallows until they turned black and sticky or snuggle up and read a stack of bedtime stories. Instead, I went right on doing exactly what I had been doing—I worked.

I worked making my grape juice popsicles from scratch, I worked to make sure that the market bread was ready by six-thirty every morning, I helped customers choose just the right sides to go with their slices of prime rib or blackened chicken, I worked to make sure we were packed and ready to go boating on the weekends. I hosted Christmas parties for 150 of our island friends, where I did all the food myself, including multiple stations with dishes of pork, beef, seafood, poultry, vegetables, and multiple desserts. I even graduated to roasting a suckling pig. I filled and decorated every inch of my holiday table myself.

And to everyone, including myself, it appeared my work in every facet of life was worth it. It was all so pretty, down to the stylish eggplant floors, because somewhere along the way I had convinced myself that pretty was everything. That how we looked from the outside was the ultimate barometer of how we were. I didn't know how to give anything else and no one seemed to ask me for anything more.

Chapter 9

MOVING TO LA
(LOWER ALABAMA)

In 1985, a hurricane hit Hilton Head Island. The funny thing about this particular hurricane was that the damage was limited to one house on South Calibogue Cay—mine. Like the barometer sitting in Mrs. Schubert's kitchen on Kenesaw Road, I could sense the change in atmosphere before the storm. It was a Thursday, and that morning, I had ridden an exercise bike with my friend and Sandy's and my real estate agent, Lottie. It was my latest form of repetitive exercise, which also included swimming and running. Most mornings after opening Truffles, I went on my ride to nowhere and finished with sweat dripping off my skin. I told Lottie, "Something's going to happen. I don't know what it is, but something's going to happen."

The day passed, and nothing happened. I had started attending an early evening membership class at a local church, which I had insisted we join because I thought Sam and David needed Sunday school, just as Keith and I had gone when we were young. However, I barely listened in class. While the minister talked about God, I thought about Truffles, recipes, or whatever else popped into my mind. That night, Sandy was waiting to pick me up. We were going to dinner, and he had a surprise: he had flown in Kay Craig, a good friend from Knoxville. Kay was a travel agent. Sandy and I had planned our resort honeymoon with her though, in typical fashion, we never ended up going.

Almost as soon as Kay arrived, Sandy blurted out the sentence, "I have some news." Scientists call the human gut the "second brain," and note that its collection of neurons is more attuned to our raw emotions than the contemplative mass of gray matter in our heads. As Sandy started to speak, my gut clenched. It didn't take long for him to deliver "the news." Morrisons, the company that had acquired Ruby Tuesday, wanted Sandy to become a full senior executive at its headquarters, located in Mobile, Alabama. And that was where we would be moving. Price would take over Truffles.

I'm sure Sandy meant for Kay's presence to lessen the shock. But it didn't. We drove in two cars to dinner at a Mexican restaurant, Sandy and the boys in one, and Kay and I in the other. Kay already knew all about our impending move. I, on the other hand, was reeling. The gas gauge on my car was on empty, so I stopped to fill it. I pumped in a full tank of regular octane. The problem was, my car was a diesel. We got about a thousand feet before the engine sputtered and died. Somehow, we found a phone, called the restaurant, and Sandy got us. The car was towed for repair. Kay flew out the next day, and so did Sandy and I.

We were off to Mobile to look at houses.

I was still in shock, but I tried to make myself feel excited about the possibilities. From my college years at Tulane in New Orleans, I loved antebellum homes. I remembered driving through Mobile once and how pretty I thought the old houses were, surrounded by corridors of live oaks dripping with Spanish moss. We did find a house, but it was a semi-new Georgian colonial on a cul-de-sac named Eaton Square with five little boys in the neighborhood.

Right after our offer was accepted, Sandy and I went to Wintzell's Oyster House in downtown Mobile to celebrate. I sat and watched a big muscular man shuck oysters, just as I used to do in New Orleans. And suddenly, I started to cry. The man looked up and said, "What you cryin' for?" And I answered, "Because I'm moving to Alabama."

For the first time, it was real. We weren't going home to Tennessee the way we had always planned to when Sam was in third or fourth grade. My children were not going to grow up where I had grown up. Instead, Alabama would be home to our boys, and everything would be different. In the nearly ten years that I had been married to Sandy, we had moved eleven times. This was the first move that did not feel like an adventure, but like a sentencing. Yet having committed ourselves to following the god of success, we had to follow him to Mobile.

We would live in Alabama for eleven years, in only four different houses—including one that we bought and sold twice. In retrospect, they would be the most formative years of our entire married life.

On the surface, my reaction was hardly rational. Hilton Head is 411 miles away from Knoxville, while Mobile is 535. But those extra 124 miles seemed to lead to another world. Tennessee is a long, thin state wedged up against North Carolina, which places it in the Upper South. Water freezes, snow falls, the land moves in a progression of geological terraces, with valleys, plateaus, and an anchoring spine of mountains. Lower

Alabama for much of its prerecorded history lay under ancient oceans and swamps; today, the city of Mobile overlooks Mobile Bay, which empties into the Gulf of Mexico. Winter is short, spring lovely, then by May, the temperature goes from hot to hotter. Mobile itself is wet, sitting under a blanket of thunderstorms, drenched in rainy, liquid heat. It is a breeding ground for giant bugs—flying roaches I used to call them—and cloying humidity that turned my hair to clumps of bushy frizz the moment it started to dry. Many days during the long summer, I'd jump in the pool or stand under the shower multiple times just to wet down my hair. But it was not simply the physical surroundings. Moving to Lower Alabama, or "LA" as Southerners like to joke, was moving to the Deep South. It was like stepping back into my mother's 1950s kitchen and opening a can of Le Sueur peas.

On our last day in Hilton Head, I hired a professional photographer to take pictures of the boys by the beach grass and sand dunes. I made Sandy promise that he would not tell anyone in Mobile that I had worked, and he agreed. In that era, it was rare for married women in Mobile, whose husbands were lawyers, doctors, or held executive positions, to have their own paying jobs and professional identities; charity drives and managing their houses and children were their primary occupations. As a new arrival to a tightly knit community, I didn't want to stick out any more than I already would.

On the drive down in June 1985, Sandy arranged for me to stop in Thomasville, Georgia. He had enrolled me in Orvis's shooting school because he knew that Alabamans hunted and he wanted me to fit in. I showed up with Sandy's twelve-gauge shotgun, which had such an awful recoil that my shoulder was bruised after a few rounds of firing at clay targets. The instructor took pity on me and gave me his girlfriend's gun to use for the duration. He need not have bothered. Being able to hunt was not going to help me fit in, unlike in Tennessee, in Alabama, women didn't hunt, except for the ones who went out in the fields during the few weeks of dove season. The rest of the time, the men went off on the weekends and the women stayed home.

Hunting season could have been a metaphor for our first year in Mobile. Sandy went off to work every day in a suit, the boys went off to school, and I stayed behind. I worked on our new house. I signed up to be David's classroom mother, plus coach baseball and be a Cub Scout leader, which were considered odd, but tolerated because coaching and scouting were volunteer jobs that few parents wanted. My Cub Scout troop built beautiful pinewood derby cars, and I had my eight-year-olds holding hammers and constructing elaborate birdhouses. I also tried joining the ladies' tennis league at the country club, buying a cute white skirt and all, but I lasted only one season. I was terrible at ladies' small talk, so I did what I had learned to do more than two decades before at my parents' house—I exited, not dropping out, I just didn't sign up again.

Truthfully, I was lonely. I had no work—Sandy couldn't give me something to run; Blackberry was still just eight part-time rooms—and no friends. One morning, I called Sandy at his office to complain about something, and, exasperated, he said, "Why are you calling me at work?" I told him, "I have no one else. So sit down, shut up, and take it like a man!" To his credit, he told me, "Okay, keep going." He was a leveler who never seemed to take anything personally, a steady ballast to my bursts of emotion and passions.

I had to find a way to live in Alabama. Seasons in Mobile

were defined not by the swings in weather, but by a reliable progression of sports and events. Fall is football, either University of Alabama or Auburn, followed by hunting season, which, unless Easter is unseasonably late, is punctuated by Mardi Gras. Mobile has the oldest Mardi Gras celebration in the country, pre-dating New Orleans, with dozens of mystic societies, multiple masqued balls, and weeks of parades that take the better part of a year to organize and design. After the celebrations, for those lucky enough to afford it, the summers are spent in a retreat "over the bay," along the resort towns that dot the Gulf Coast, where houses get passed down for generations and which fish market you buy your shrimp from is the subject of significant discussion and debate.

That first year, I had solved the what-to-do-for-Mardi-Gras problem by going skiing. Sandy solved what to do about Mobile's sticky wet summer. When he bought our house on Eaton Square, he insisted that we also find a second house over on the bay.

We drove through a collection of little towns—Spanish Fort, Daphne, Fairhope, Point Clear—in search of the right spot. My choice was between beach towns with sand, sun, and water and the slightly more inland spaces with trees and gardens and shady yards. My favorite of them all was Point Clear, where the coastline hooks down into the bay, the winds race over the water, and the sun drops low at dusk. At night, you can see the faint glow of Mobile and if you look up, bright arcs of stars. Sandy found and purchased a clapboard cottage that we nicknamed the Little Bay House. We put in a dock, what everyone else around us called a "wharf," and tied up a boat for waterskiing. From the house, we could walk to the Grand Hotel, where most families had a swim membership and used the pool. Sam and David were our ambassadors to the area, always out exploring the neighborhood and making friends.

Now, instead of worrying about a restaurant and a bistro market, I thought about houses, gardens, family meals, and entertaining, and threw myself into every part. I fried chicken and made corn and salads and baked cakes and cookies, which I also turned into homemade ice cream sandwiches. I rolled dough and filled pies and served everything family-style on picnic tables. Much like when we were first married, I issued impromptu invitations. All kinds of people came: people I didn't know, friends of friends, or someone's cousins or distant in-laws.

Because I did everything myself, I started to get a reputation for food, in that easy one-line way of saying, "Oh, Kreis Beall, she's the one who loves to cook." When *Southern Living* magazine was scouting around for a place to take pictures to accompany an article on the Alabama coast, an editor called me to see if they could use our house. They staged a photo shoot and alongside the article, they ran a picture of our living room, a distant image of our house, and also a picture of Sam and David, two of their friends, and our dogs, down by the water. I was living what looked like a perfect life.

By the end of that first year, the state I never wanted to move to and the place where I didn't fit in had given me the gift of my vocation: my life became about creating home. It was far more than just the look of our house though, it was really a philosophy of life and home. The home I created in Alabama became the incubator for the home that I would one day work to create at Blackberry. It would become the place where my children established their own definitions of home. It would be a place that Sandy and I unabashedly loved long after we left it.

Because Sandy was one of the most successful men in town,

I was on many women's invite lists. I might be a poor joiner, but politeness and protocol dictated that no one shut the door; I just occasionally got bumped by the hinged screen. So on a super-sticky July day, when the air was as liquid as the water, I ended up at a ladies' tubing party on the south side of the bay in Point Clear. The women all gathered at Kitty's wharf to fly about in inner tubes pulled by motorboats, or simply wade in.

I wore a one-piece tank suit covered by a T-shirt, and old tennis shoes on my feet. Every other woman was dressed much the same, except for one. This woman looked like a Roman goddess, tall, bone-thin, her suit covered by a meticulously tied sarong, her neck accented by silver earrings, and her platinum hair twisted into an elegant bun. Big sunglasses hid her eyes.

I watched her standing on the wharf, walked over and said, without any polite small talk, "Do you ever let your hair down and get in the water?" She turned slightly, looked at me, and without saying a word, untied her sarong, let down her hair, and jumped in. One of the other women standing nearby eyed me in half horror. "I can't believe you said that to Camille."

I replied, "Why? What do you say to her?"

When Camille emerged, dripping wet and grinning, I knew we were going to be fast friends, both of us completely at home, just jumping in without looking.

Chapter 10

SOUTHERN COOKING

Mobile was small. Camille's sister lived by us on Eaton Square, and Camille was building her own new house a few blocks away. Camille was the only "C" in her family. Her husband, Happy Luscher, was a doctor, and they had a son named Hayes, and two daughters, Hebard and Hill. Today, her grandchildren call her "Camel," and she takes pride in that, too. Each summer, the Luschers rented the same house over on the bay, which we called the Brown House, where Camille brought her linens and spruced up what might have otherwise been a very plain place. There were only three or four young mothers who spent their summers along the boardwalk. Our children were always outside, so we were always outside; in that easy way, friendship found us. That, and a boat.

Waterskiing was part of life on the bay, and when Camille realized that her summer babysitter didn't know how, she decided to give her lessons. "Does anybody know how to drive a boat?" she asked one afternoon. "I do," I answered. Of course, I had never driven a boat, but I thought, *I can drive a car, and my boys know how to drive boats. How hard can it be?* The next morning, I asked David, who was ten, to help me get the boat down out of the lift, take the hooks off, and turn on the engine.

With the boat in the water, I figured I could manage forward and reverse, and fortunately the boat was already facing forward. All I had to do was to get close enough to the wharf that someone could grab the sides and pull us in to dock. My trial-and-error boating got us on the bay for waterskiing, where Camille's sitter wobbled on her skis, then to the Grand Hotel for lunch by the pool, followed by a water tour of all the pretty houses. We got back just as the sun was starting to set, and after a hard bump against the wharf, I said, "All right, everybody hop out and help me dock." With the boat secured, in my jauntiest voice I said, "That was fun. Thanks for all the help. I've never done this before." Camille arched an eyebrow and then she threw back her head and laughed. She knew how to dock. Truth be told, she probably could have driven the boat, too.

I had guessed right from the beginning. Camille was different from many women in Mobile and not simply because of her appearance. She worked as an interior designer and had a part interest in a French antiques store. I learned a lot about houses and design from her. She would tell clients that it might take her a couple of months to finish a project because she had to interrupt her work for whatever her children and husband needed and for holidays or school and family events. Sometimes she referred new clients to designers in other cities because she could see that they, the men especially but sometimes their wives, too, didn't really want to take advice or direction from a "local woman."

Camille had lived in Tennessee when Happy did his medical residency in Memphis. She remembered the time Happy was invited to go hunting with a group of men and she told him that Tennessee is different from Alabama. In Tennessee, she said, the women join their husbands. Happy waved her off and then returned chagrined. He was the only man in the hunting party to show up without his wife. In fact, most times when she told that story, Camille would add that in Tennessee, women even *own* the hunting camps.

For Sandy and me, Alabama hunting season was the toughest code to crack. It seemed that anyone who was considered a *gentleman* in Mobile belonged to a hunting camp, where the men would go each weekend to hunt, eat, and drink, and school their sons in their traditions. It was unacceptable not to have some combination of frozen venison—steaks, ground meat, or stew cubes—in the freezer. Hunting camps are exactly what they sound like: camps, often very rustic sleeping lodges, in the middle of forests or perhaps along a river. They are nestled in empty tracts of land populated by deer, quail, and wild turkeys. Our first year, Sandy wasn't invited to join any established hunting camps, so he went off and rented his own, an old sharecropper's cabin that was part of a larger estate.

I made our cabin look like how I imagined a very rustic-minded Ralph Lauren would have outfitted his hunting camp, if it had been one large room, with a fireplace, a single bedroom, and a bathroom that was about four feet by four feet, with a tiny plastic shower, a wall sink, and a commode. The six-by-eight kitchen was slightly larger, and I pasted new linoleum on its floor. There was also a porch, where I put the turkey roaster, and finally a "bonus room" for the kids, with wall-to-wall carpet, bunk beds, and a pool table. Sandy, Sam, David, and I would pack up the coolers and head there on the weekends. While I decorated and cooked the meals, Sandy took Sam and David into the woods to sit and wait for deer, most of the time with his briefcase and a stack of work in tow. There were long stretches of sitting and waiting, and Sandy has never been one for long periods of waiting around with very little to do.

While for Sandy, hunting and fishing fell somewhere in the category of duties rather than a genuine love, Sam loved both. David was more like Sandy—they went through the motions because it was so very much a part of being a guy in Alabama and indeed much of the South. I also took David to sit silently in the woods and wait for a target to amble past. I came to appreciate that, after a week of busyness, these weekends were just the four of us, with no television and no telephone. One weekend, Sandy read aloud from the classic Robert Ruark book *The Old Man and the Boy*, about a ten-year-old and his grandfather. Eight-year-old David piped up to ask Sandy to read the story about the eight-year-old boy, which Sandy proceeded to do by reading the exact same story and making the little boy eight.

Our second year in Mobile, Sandy was invited to join a men's hunting camp, where he took the boys, although he kept the same routine of carrying his briefcase and his financial printouts into the woods. When Sam saw his dad gathering up his stack of papers, he would roll his eyes and say, "Dad, don't let anybody see that."

Camille told me that I must not give up the lease on our little camp and proposed that we make it into a women's hunting camp, which we did. We named it the floral-sounding Hedgerose, in stark contrast to the men's camp, called Kidds' Graveyard after a headstone on the land. When the men packed their cars with their gear and provisions, we packed our cars as well. Hedgerose became a place for Camille and me and her daughters, our friend Joanne Cooper, whose husband, David, ran much of Mardi Gras, and any other women we cared to invite. As my boys were drawn into the orbit of Alabama men, I was grateful for these women. Fall and winter hunting life was like summer bay life where there was a rhythm and routine. They were the two places I thrived outside of work.

We told the men they could come over to our camp if they asked permission first, but often they would just show up, especially around dinnertime, because our food was always better than anything they had cooked. Eventually, Sandy and I, the Luschers, and the Coopers started having Thanksgiving at Hedgerose, out on picnic tables piled high with food, and in the spring, Easter egg hunts in the grass and brush.

Between the hunting camp and the bay house, for the better part of a decade, most of my weekends began and ended with packing and unpacking coolers of food, clothing, changes of towels and linens. Church was part and parcel of the life around us, but I never worried or much thought about missing services on Sundays; I was too caught up in making breakfast and rounding up laundry. The boys had chapel in school, and we said a pleasant grace before meals. During my ritual period of trying new things, I had tried a woman's Bible study, but when the leader said that I wouldn't know Sandy in heaven, I dropped out.

Sandy was my husband and closest friend—he was the person I had followed to Mobile, and I wasn't signing on to anyone's view of a heaven where we would be strangers to each other. It was difficult enough to live with segregated hunting camps and men who moved in one sphere while expecting their wives to live in another.

*   *   *

Without much planning, I had found a new vocation: I threw myself into making my physical world more beautiful, into my garden, my cooking, my entertaining. This bolstered my reputation as a hostess, not because I was always great at what I did, but because I did it over and over. Sometimes the simple fact of consistently making a thing happen is enough to be seen as having a touch of magic.

After seeing the *Southern Living* bay house photo shoot, a designer I knew in passing recommended me for a magazine piece on entertaining. Then I got a call from a writer who wanted to do a story about me for a monthly feature on home cooks in *Bon Appétit*. She interviewed me and wrote the article, which was centered around creating a Fourth of July picnic, and they accepted it. The only thing missing were my recipes. I sat down and wrote out what I made all the time: fried chicken, marinated corn on the cob, West Indies crab salad, peach pie, ice cream, and faxed them in, thinking, *I hope these recipes are okay.* I had no idea they were going to be tested in the magazine's professional kitchen. Everything made the cut except for the West Indies crab salad, which mixes fresh blue crab, onions, vinegar, water, salt, and pepper, and often looks kind of gray. It tastes great, but it's not photogenic.

Because of the quirks of magazine schedules and long lead times, all these stories appeared close together. It's amazing how a few little things, just a bit of publicity, can make people think you're known for something.

It was my first taste of independent recognition, and I liked it. Sandy's professional success in the restaurant world and my personal success in the home sphere seemed like the perfect complement. I didn't have to work to establish any deep relationships; I just had to work to make an attractive dinner and set a pretty table. Home was my business, and all I talked was business.

The morning after I faxed in my recipes to *Bon Appétit,* I left to attend a cooking class at Martha Stewart's house in Connecticut. I never went to a culinary school where professional chefs are trained, but I couldn't resist a good cooking school from the moment I finished Kathleen Barron's in Knoxville. In January 1978, during the early days of Blackberry, the Greenbrier resort had offered a very enticing cooking school. David was scheduled to be delivered by C-section on February 1. I told my doctor about the cooking school, and he said one word: "No." I ignored him and made my reservation despite the fact that it would mean driving through mountains and likely snow. Before I left, I made sure to study the map to see exactly where the hospitals were located along the way from Knoxville to White Sulphur Springs, West Virginia. At the Greenbrier, our class learned a different meal every day, and the last meal was held in the Presidential Suite, which had an upstairs and a downstairs with a private dining room, featuring fireplaces at each end and a long table. Dinner was served on the presidential gold service, with violin players in the background. It was completely over the top.

I measured all cooking schools against the Greenbrier until I went to Martha Stewart's a decade later. I'd followed her since her cookbook *Entertaining* was released in 1982. I cooked every recipe in that book, I read her pieces in magazines, and I subscribed to her newsletter, which is how I learned about the cooking school at her house, Turkey Hill, in Connecticut.

After nearly forty years, it's easy, perhaps, to forget how absolutely transformational Martha was. At a time when women were trying to find their way in the workplace, she professionalized the world at home. By making her home a business, she made it okay for any woman to make her home into her business. People can argue about Martha's aspirational lifestyle and perfectionism, but in her own way, she expanded everyone's choices. And for women in my age group, women who did not have a visible pathway to combine staying home with a professional life, Martha gave us a template for looking at the choices we had made as professional choices, ones that involved skill and effort and ability as surely as if we had put on a skirted suit and carried a briefcase to an office.

At most cooking schools, if you learn four or five things in a day, it's a huge success. Martha was such an overachiever that we came away with twelve or more new ideas and skills each day. After a morning in her catering kitchen, we went to her house for lunch, toured her gardens, and learned about homekeeping and gardening. I immediately decided two things: Martha was becoming so famous that she was not going to be doing this much longer, and I was going to sign up for the next school she offered, which started in one month.

This time, I convinced friends to go with me, including Camille. The session started with us sitting alert in Martha's perfectly organized, gleaming test kitchen in Westport, with its big restaurant stove, which looked like it had never experienced a burned meal or a failed pâte brisée. Everyone in the class was in awe and afraid to speak. Martha gave her opening speech and then paused to ask if there were any questions. Camille raised her hand and in her perfect, slow-rolling Mobile voice, said, "I have that exact same stove. How *do you* turn it on?"

Martha almost died, but the ice was broken.

When we got home, I cooked everything we had learned that week. After eighty hours of Martha Stewart, I was the opposite of intimidated. I believed if she could do it, so could I.

Chapter 11

PROMISE ME A ROSE GARDEN

When we arrived in Mobile, I had dreamed of finding a beautiful old antebellum house. I quickly learned, however, that those houses almost never came on the market. They were either sold privately or more often were handed down within families, generation after generation. But occasionally a classic home was listed for sale in and around Point Clear. The advice Sandy got was not to deliberate or negotiate, just buy it on the spot, because otherwise the house would be gone.

Our second year in Mobile we got a call about a house that might, possibly, perhaps be coming on the market. It was the second-oldest house in Point Clear, right on the water, a few lots down from the Grand Hotel. Sandy said, "Let's go take a look." It wasn't formally listed, which meant we could walk around the house but not go in. The house was blue and sat on pilings so that water from a storm surge could flow underneath. It was surrounded by live oaks, huge azaleas, and a tree-lined driveway. When we peered in the windows, we saw it was only two rooms wide, but the pilings and the high ceilings with full-length windows made everything look tall. Pressing my face against the glass, I could see the original wooden interiors and the beautiful patina of the old floors. It had all the romance of an antebellum home, a double-wide lot, and double porch with sweeping views of the bay. A white gate opened to the narrow boardwalk with a beautiful wharf beyond. It had a playhouse and a garage building that could be turned into a guesthouse, and there was space for the proverbial "engagement ring" pool. I think Sandy made an offer that afternoon.

Did I realize this day was nearly as life-altering as when Sandy pulled up in his silver Jaguar with two icy highball glasses? Or the day we walked in the door of the main house at Blackberry Farm? I'm sure I didn't. It was about our twentieth house together. I had almost stopped counting.

Three decades later, the magic of that home still holds our family's heart.

We did not choose Rose Bay because we were in search of a challenge, or needed to move, or had calculated its investment possibilities; we bought it out of love.

Its old, slightly creaky floors welcomed all manner of damp, sun-drenched children trailing crab pots, sand, and water from the bay. It was a place where I could put quilts over picnic tables and invite neighbors to a last-minute dinner party simply because I had too much ripe squash on the vine or I had not been able to resist a boatman's overflowing pile of freshly caught shrimp or crab. Something about the house's big porch and oversize doors made me want to throw them open and share. I didn't care who came or whether everything matched, and there was an incredible freedom in that unplanned ease. Without consciously realizing it, I had finally created my own version of Mammy's "feel good" home. It was the home where we were all happy simply being at home, where no one craved to leave for the weekend. So many evenings and Sunday afternoons, Sandy and I sat in our rockers on the porch. We shared food, cocktails, and stories, and forged friendships that would last for decades. I still count my bay friends as among my best friends.

At Rose Bay, Sandy and I lived downstairs while the boys had the run of the second floor. Their bedrooms opened into a great room, off of which sat a big screened porch with a Ping-Pong table. Sam organized running tournaments that went on night after night. In the pre-smartphone age, summers existed without schedules or cars. We turned the boys loose in the morning to swim, fish, or take a boat out to water-ski. In our own form of shared bay parenting, moms along the boardwalk watched whatever pack of children was racing by. "Easy, safe, and independent" was how David would look back on those summers and those years.

We never had to think about what we would do if life got hard. We never imagined living another life.

About a year after we moved in, Rose Bay formally embraced its name. Years before when we first lived at Blackberry, I had seen a photograph in the Wayside seed catalog for a charming cutting garden. Excited, I ordered all the packets, sowed the seeds, watered, fertilized, and waited for my lovely cutting garden to emerge. Needless to say, what eventually came up didn't look like what was in the catalog.

In Point Clear, I developed a renewed case of garden lust. I started by planting one thousand parrot tulips. But as I looked out on a spot of land behind the garage that we had renovated to become a guesthouse, I dreamed of something much bigger:

an English-style rose garden. After Mammy passed away in 1988 and left me a small inheritance, I decided to invest it in roses so I would always have an abundance of flowers to cut.

I hired a garden designer whom I had heard speak at Martha Stewart's and spent months reading everything I could find on roses. I studied genealogy and read about the differences between hybrid tea roses and antique roses. I had to learn how to get the soil right and how to tend the roses while they were growing. Late fall or early winter is the best time to plant, which is done by placing the bare root in the soil. I wouldn't know if they had survived until the leaves came out. Then the buds would follow. By May, they will burst into bloom. Not all roses will make it. The bloom is only the first step. They require serious care, fertilizing to keep the pests away, soil that is neither too damp nor too dry, and pruning in the fall, so they will flourish and regrow.

In November, more than two hundred bare-root roses arrived. After the holes were dug, the garden looked like a tiny burial ground, with row after row of solitary sticks. By late spring, I basked in my rows of blousy pink, yellow, and white roses. While the blooms lasted, my garden overflowed.

No sooner did those flowers take than another dormant place began to put out new shoots: Blackberry Farm was calling.

Gary Doyle, our manager, had phoned Sandy and me and said in his low-key way that the next time we were in Tennessee, we should come by because the garage was falling down. Typical of us: within twenty-four hours, we were tearing down the garage to build something bigger. By 1989, the bank leases were long gone, but Blackberry had developed a loyal clientele from those years. People who had come to play poker or for small company retreats wanted to return with their friends and family. We hosted what we dubbed "Big Chill" weekends. With those and other small events, Blackberry was operating on auto-pilot, sometimes losing a bit of money, but mostly breaking even. What had changed was that over the years, we, along with some partners, had been able to put several thousand acres of the surrounding land in trust, so Blackberry had grown to 4,200 acres, all of it in a conservancy never to be developed.

Sandy was in the hospitality business; I was in the home hospitality business. For us, a garage was never just a garage. A small change was the chance to make a big change. Our boys were growing, and it seemed like the right time to start paying more attention to our "third child."

Looking at the collapsing structure, we asked Gary, "What do the guests want?" And he answered, "The guests want exactly what we have now. They just want more of it." Then we asked, "What do you need?" Gary had an answer for that, too. He said, "More rooms, because we don't have enough rooms to fill the number of requests." So that was what we gave him—a guesthouse that was almost a duplicate of the main house and an expanded dining room. The same Blackberry, just more of it. We hired an architect who worked for the firm that had designed the original house and got to work. Right after we started in 1988, the stock market crashed and Ruby Tuesday stock went from twenty-five dollars a share to eleven dollars. We couldn't stop the project, but we had to shrink it, so we made the bathrooms and bedrooms smaller, a decision we would come to regret for years. I ran back and forth from Mobile to Blackberry, to oversee the work and design the rooms, putting thousands of miles on my minivan. Every time I learned something new about cooking or gardens or decorating in Mobile, I would try it out at Blackberry.

Long before *Downton Abbey,* I designed this renovation to be a 1990 version of an English country house, with flowered chintz, plaids, and stripes, featherbeds on the mattresses—which were very unusual at the time—and a matelassé bedspread (thank you, Camille) on top and a fluffy comforter spread across the bottom, in a layered, rather feminine look, which is ironic because I'm not particularly feminine in my aesthetic or design. Sandy wanted me to buy everything in bulk, but I said no—each room had to be different, with different fabrics, different furniture, making each space "one of a kind." I took the living room carpet and draperies bought for what would have been our Knoxville dream house, which we sold after we moved to Mobile, and installed them in the inn's living room. I hung our antique brass chandelier in the dining room. If Blackberry felt like stepping into someone's home, that's because in part it was.

If I had a vision, I was certain I could execute it. If a low, damp spot in the land needed a pond to become beautiful, our team and I built a small, glistening pond ringed by reeds and cattails, with a perfect white boathouse and a canoe tied up at the dock. We had the pond dredged with a backhoe, our talented architect drew the blueprints, and our builder sank the footings and built the boathouse from the ground up. The resulting tableau looked as if it had stood on that exact spot for at least a century, periodically refreshed with a good coat of paint. I was sure it was what Nature would have designed if she had time to spare and access to a good builder and backhoe.

When people in Mobile asked me where I had been, I told the truth. More often than not, their response was "Why didn't you ever tell us about Blackberry?" I wanted to be a smart mouth and say "Because you never asked." (It took me decades to outgrow the sharp-tongued side of me that I had visited on Keith when we were young. Truth be told, I'm still working on the last pieces of it.) Most women in our social world wouldn't think to ask, while most men never considered the possibility of wives working. But I just smiled and said it wasn't a big deal, and the conversation would roll on to sports or hunting or Mardi Gras.

In 1990, we opened the expanded Blackberry, hoping guests would follow. That same year, Keith called to say she was checking herself into rehab and getting sober. Without a pause, I said we would take her children for as long as she needed.

My household doubled to four boys: Abby in ninth, Sam in eighth, David in seventh, and Dylan in sixth. It wasn't as much as it sounded. Already during the summer, Abby and Dylan often spent weeks at Rose Bay. They had been absorbed into epic games of capture the flag and put on the Ping-Pong roster. On Domino's pizza night, we simply ordered more. The four boys played, wrestled, and fought like siblings. I vividly remember one night when Sam walked in and dumped a cup of water on Abby's head. Abby dumped his own cup in retaliation and that dissolved into a wrestling match, that resulted in a broken glass and Abby bleeding everywhere from a deep cut on his arm. Sandy and I were asleep, but one of the boys woke us. Sandy was first upstairs. He looked at Abby and the blood and passed out. I got Sandy to sit up and threw Abby in my car to rush him to the ER. Once I was gone, Sandy passed out again. The boys called Camille's husband, Happy, who was a doctor. He raced over and had Sandy bundled off in an ambulance, worried he was having a heart attack. Instead it was a vasovagal syncope— Sandy passes out at the sight of blood. It was Beall family night in the ER.

Everyone lived under the same roof and by the same rules. If one boy misbehaved, all the boys suffered the consequences. Sandy usually meted out punishments in the morning but told them it was coming before bed, making the dread even more effective than the reprimand. But the camaraderie was equally strong. There was never "our two children and their two cousins," or a weighty sense of obligation. Sandy never once said "your sister's sons." They were all ours. We had the space to give, and the unity in giving made us stronger.

But for us, it was also easy. We had four bedrooms upstairs, so each boy could automatically have a room. We had plenty of money to provide. The fridge was stocked, and everyone had the right gear for fishing, hunting, and boating. I ran my house like an innkeeper—physical wants anticipated and gratified. Sam would say later that during those years, he thought of me as "supermom," but I look back and wonder about that.

We were busy, living amidst a constant flurry of cooking, hosting, renovating, decorating, Sandy's trips for work, my trips to Blackberry. Life was rich and time raced by. And while I know that we loved each other, looking back, I can't help but wonder if I mistook proximity for intimacy? I worked hard to nurture our bodies with food, and our lives with beauty, but I wonder if I missed nourishing our souls and our hearts.

GROWING A GARDEN

When I began gardening, I thought it would be like following a recipe: Buy these ingredients, follow the directions, and I will have a garden that looks just like the picture in the magazine or on the seed packet. But that is not exactly how it happens. My first garden at Blackberry didn't come up. I sowed the seeds in the right spot, followed every direction, checked the sun, and nothing grew. But despite that failure, something in me said, You must try again. I kept believing that my next effort would take and my elusive garden dreams would be realized.

For four decades, gardens have taught me about successes and failures and about things that are beyond our control, such as pests, blight, drought, or too much rain. They have also taught me about constant care. You cannot do a few things and walk away for months at a time. Gardens require a steady level of repetitive maintenance and specific tasks at specific times of the year, like feeding, pruning, and deadheading. I think about the loss embodied in removing the dead growth and the stems and branches of the previous season. Often it looks as if you are killing the plant. Then, come spring, the once shorn plant is healthier and fuller than ever before, precisely because you cut out the disease and the dead growth.

Beyond pruning, so much of the rhythm of a garden is a mirror for the rhythm of our own lives. Gardeners need to have patience, persistence, and humility. You have to select plants that are suited to your soil and your climate, to be open to what will thrive, rather than to impose your plant vision on the environment. You need to choose what you can maintain. At age one-hundred, Sam Beall, Sandy's father, still has a vegetable garden.

His plot has gotten a bit smaller and is now about twelve by sixteen. When he turned ninety-three, he started having one of his grandsons till the soil. But he has never given up his garden. His and Mary Anne's signature gift was live plants they had grown, something of them that would come up year after year. Many of my friends give freshly cut flowers from their yards, but the message is the same: Here is something beautiful that I have worked to grow and want to share with you.

The most beautiful garden I have been given was planted not by a garden professional but by my friend Susan Wojnar. For years, I had a dog named Buddy, whom I adored. When he died, I buried him at Blackberry. I got a small plaque, but what I really wanted was a mound of daffodils, to come up bright and hopeful, year after year, just like Buddy. He passed away in the summer, so there were no bulbs to be found and it was the wrong time to plant them. Susan waited out the seasons until January, when it was daffodil planting time. Then she dug up the soil and secured the bulbs. I didn't know what she had done until they poked up their green shoots and bloomed. Those flowers said everything about friendship and love as they turned their yellow faces toward the early-spring sun.

Chapter 12

BACK TO BLACKBERRY

The first time I read the Bible as an adult was when I found myself without my children.

Growing up, no one in my household gave much thought to religion. My parents came from two different denominations, Methodist and Episcopalian, but they chose our church, Sequoyah Presbyterian, for convenience—it was a short walk. My father enrolled us in Sunday School, and the four of us dutifully worshiped together at Christmas and Easter. Thanks to our mom, Keith and I always arrived looking like perfectly groomed little girls, in tie-back dresses with crinoline petticoats (mine was so itchy I cut it out with my father's fingernail scissors) or smocked cotton shifts paired with Capezio ballet shoes. We carefully ate our communion wafers and sipped our Welch's grape juice communion "wine" from thimble-size cups.

In the summer, I went to Bible school, and I remember it to this day because it was so boring. We colored, and I learned that Jesus was born, then He died, and that He had two holidays. I silently wondered where He was on the other big days, like

Thanksgiving, Fourth of July, and Valentine's Day. If He was there with Santa and the Easter Bunny, why not with turkeys and fireworks and red hearts as well?

Otherwise, I didn't have much to say to God during that narrow window on Sunday mornings. I never envisioned I might one day open the Bible, searching and eager for the words within.

Keith had often told me that I should be careful about going away on solo trips, because invariably, I would return to find that Sandy had bought a new car or even another house. After one long weekend, I learned that Sandy had visited two boarding schools for the boys without me.

I had long worried about Sam's progress reports from his school in Mobile, and we had talked about boarding school for all four boys, ours and Keith's. Sandy did his best to convince me that they should attend the McCallie School, a Christian boarding school in Chattanooga, Tennessee. Sandy has always been persuasive, and when I visited the school, I was impressed. My original "You're kidding me," response became a "Yes." The truth was he had basically already enrolled them.

I packed four trunks and sent them off with their blue blazers and khaki pants, dress shirts and ties. Believing, and having been persuaded, that it was the right thing for them, I never even stopped to consider how I would feel after they were gone.

Overnight, I became an empty nester. My friends' lives and activities still revolved around their children, while suddenly my day-to-day job as a mother had been terminated. I felt unmoored and unneeded. The boys had school. Sandy traveled the entire week for work. The only person whose life had been upended was me. No one seemed to understand, even I didn't to-tally understand how I could be so sad over a decision I had agreed to.

So I repeated a pattern I had followed my entire life: I found an exit strategy. I left Rose Bay and fled to my other child, Blackberry Farm. When there was a problem I couldn't solve, I avoided it; I pivoted and headed in a different direction. I told Sandy I was going to the newly expanded Blackberry to work. He could fly in to Knoxville and see me there. I moved to the original farmhouse on the property, down by the creek, across from a tiny peeling–white paint shed, and immersed myself in Blackberry's day-to-day operations.

Sending the boys to boarding school was the first major personal dispute Sandy and I had in our married life. We did not fight over how to raise our children. We did not fight over our household money because there had usually been plenty, and even when there wasn't, we lived our lives in exactly the same way.

We did not fight over travel or moving. Up until this point, about the only things we had disagreed over were Blackberry or occasionally a detail in a house renovation. I was very vision focused, and Sandy was very cost focused. I would fight for what I thought was best for the spirit of Blackberry, while Sandy would fight for what was the best deal for Blackberry. People would see us argue in meetings and then we'd go to lunch and talk like nothing had happened. I'd hear, "I thought you were mad at him." And I'd say, "No, I'm not mad, I just want what I think is best for Blackberry." It wasn't personal, it was business, and that was part of the problem. We didn't have any ability to deal with personal conflict.

Our Blackberry disagreements always resolved themselves,

and that made this struggle over the boys and our home life even harder. My hurt feelings and sense of loss were not going to be assuaged by simply working harder. Instead, they festered. Sandy would fly in for the weekends and we were polite with each other. Then he would fly out, but nothing was resolved. We were flat, just going through the motions.

I picked up the Bible out of pure proximity. It was sitting on one of my tables.

I wasn't a person who looked to books, any type of books, for help, unless it was to find a new recipe or a bit of decorating inspiration. I had never even read the jacket of a self-help book. The title of the most popular one at the time, *Men Are from Mars, Women Are from Venus,* was a turnoff. Although my sister had been to rehab, I never considered a psychologist. My parents dismissed people who set foot in a psychiatrist's or psychologist's office as "shrink freaks," and I wasn't much more enlightened. But I had always heard people talking about receiving comfort from the "Good Book," so I decided to give it a try.

I'm here to tell you that reading the Bible without a guide is hard. Really hard. I doggedly made it through the verses, passively waiting for the curtain to be magically pulled back and a great revelation to descend on me, or at the least a neat and tidy answer. It was like expecting housekeeping to knock if I simply hung the Please Make Up This Room sign. (One of my Blackberry improvements was to order cute embroidered pillows for guests' doors that read "Go Away.") But nothing came. Nor could I do as Psalm 51 asked, "Create in me a clean heart."

Instead, I got angrier: at Sandy, and at myself for being so weak that I couldn't just work this out. I was furious that while I had left for a few days Sandy had made such a life-changing decision for all of us. I never considered that this was how we had made most of what should have been joint decisions: independently of each other. We passed a large chunk of that year ignoring our problems. When we did finally address them, it was, ironically enough, triggered by business.

Sandy was a member of the YPO, Young Presidents Organization, and several times a year, he and other young executives in his group would meet to talk about business and about life. He mentioned that I had left our home in Alabama. One of the other men in his group told him about a psychologist team in Texas, Richard and Nancy Lee, who did high-impact, intensive counseling for one week. It was a set time commitment: fly in and fly out. Perfect for busy executives. This man had done it with his wife, and he said something like "You should look into it, Beall."

That was all it took. Sandy made an appointment, and we went. I met with Nancy Lee and Sandy met with Richard, and then we met together to talk. It did help. It opened up lines of communication.

Sandy and I agreed to bring the boys home, although interestingly, years later, he recalls their boarding school year quite differently from me, saying that Sam wanted to go and the other boys followed. The terms were that the boys could come home after a year. With good grades and having become better students, it was "all happy," and a "win-win," in his words.

That is an excellent summary for a boardroom meeting. But a marriage is different. My own memories and emotions from that time are so different.

We left the Texas counseling sessions with a list of relationship fixes, much like a punch list after a renovation. We had to do things like always take a call from your spouse, no matter what you are doing. Sandy would always take my call, someone would always come find me whenever he called, because this was the era before cell phones. There were other little things on our to-dos, like each time someone returned after traveling to make sure to hug each other and say, "Welcome home." But these were mechanical steps. They did not address the deeper issues that were festering in our marriage. We, or at least I, thought that we had successfully completed marriage boot-camp, but in actuality, not much was truly different. We were both still focused less on the present and more on checking off our next accomplishments.

Success is a great patch-and-glue job. It covers up so many underlying cracks with minimal effort.

At first, with the boys home and all of us living back in Mobile and Point Clear, I naively assumed that we would resume the same rhythm in our lives. But things had shifted, and each of us had grown more independent, and with that, a little more apart.

Sam was old enough to drive, so I surrendered my role as the on-call chauffeur. Each day he drove a car full of kids, including Camille's, to school. He made them listen in silence to the *News and Comment* program by the folksy-sounding announcer Paul Harvey on the radio—they would leave when it started and pull into the parking lot as Paul signed off. I never knew until years later that Sam liked Paul Harvey, even though I was at home with my radio on, doing the exact same thing. I simply waved goodbye when they pulled away.

In his cousin Abby's words, "Sam always had a master plan." Just as he ran Ping-Pong tournaments and capture the flag games by laying out the ground rules and then managing the players, he began to apply that same single-minded focus to his life. At the end of his junior year at UMS Wright in Mobile, he announced he was going to run for student body president. When I asked why, he said because his grades were awful: "I don't have anything on my résumé to get into college, and I need something." I said, "When's the election?" He replied, "Friday." I asked him if there was anything I could do, and he said no. He won, even though he was the kid who stuttered when he had to speak in public, and being student body president required him to get up and speak before the school every week.

My sphere was running the social events at our house. I liked having the kids' friends over or hosting the senior graduation party, which we held at Rose Bay with a few other parents to chaperone and a couple of off-duty police officers at the end of the driveway to make sure no one left. But unlike when they were younger, I didn't get involved in the school or go to hear Sam speak, although I would show up on the sidelines for sporting events, Sam's football games, and David's tennis matches. I did my own thing and didn't psychologically participate in my boys' lives. I equated the functioning of our family with the functioning of my house: if it was well run, we were happy or so it seemed.

Sandy and I decided on our own fresh start in the way that we knew best: with a renovation of our home Rose Bay. We split the responsibilities based on our areas of expertise: he would oversee the construction and I would handle the interior design.

In typical Sandy style, he gave me an offer I couldn't refuse.

He repeatedly suggested that we move over to the bay full time, while we were living in our weekday house in Mobile. I said no a few times before it finally dawned on me. "You've sold this house, haven't you?" I asked. He answered simply, "Yes."

The redo of Rose Bay took a little over a year. When the movers left, Sandy and I celebrated with a dinner by candlelight. In that moment, we both believed this would be our last home, not forever, but at least for a very long time. I could not have known, looking into those dancing flames, that the clock was already ticking.

It was hard to disagree or to stay mad at Sandy, because he was so willing to share his business wisdom and financial success. He paid for my sister's children's education, he paid for Keith to go to counseling in Texas, he paid for our houses, and for Blackberry. What he knew best was how to work harder to give more financially. Like Sandy, I, too, came to rely on work and outward markers of success to fulfill me; it was where I took my heart and soul to be renewed. Sandy and I were best friends, forged together by work. Even our hobby of moving houses, renovating, and decorating related to work. Pursuing a house, the effort to get the best deal, was what Sandy loved. He has always been athletic. He could have devoted himself to tennis or golf, but his true passion was work. It was easy to become a workaholic alongside him, because frankly it was rewarding, not only the enjoyment of success, but because there was an emotional payoff in a job well done.

So there we sat, having a celebration dinner because Rose Bay was now renovated from the ground up. It was also a celebration that Blackberry was coming into its own and being recognized. Our financial bank was full, but our emotional bank was being emptied. We just didn't know it.

* * *

The magazine coverage I had gotten and my reputation at Rose Bay landed me a position as a contributing editor for *Southern Accents,* which focused on the art of entertaining. I loved it, but I didn't have enough time to devote to the magazine along with the Blackberry expansion. After a year, I called my editor and told her that I needed to step down, but would she be interested in coming to visit Blackberry Farm? It was a long shot, in part because although Blackberry sat at the edge of the Smoky Mountains, in the 1990s, most people weren't eager to vacation in eastern Tennessee. When it came to the rest of the country's ideas on ranking sophisticated, elegant destinations, our region was somewhere between *The Waltons* and *Deliverance.* But my editor, Katherine Pearson, said yes. Gary and Bernadette Doyle rolled out the red carpet, and she was enchanted. Katherine was also switching publications, from *Southern Accents* to *Southern Living,* the magazine with the largest circulation in the South, and she wanted to feature Blackberry in *Southern Living*'s Christmas issue. She said that Blackberry embodied everything that *Southern Living* wrote about: food, home, family, travel, holidays, and the region.

I was momentarily over-overjoyed at this publicity coup, then I was beset by full-blown panic. For years, Sandy, the boys, and I had gone to Blackberry for Christmas. But family stockings hanging by the fireplace would not suffice for *Southern Living.* This article was a huge opportunity for Blackberry, so everything had to be perfect. I called Camille as well as Joanne Cooper, who had spent so many weekends with us at the hunting camp, and asked them to please come help. For more than a week, we worked around the clock, decorating each room. I sent Camille and Joanne out to dig up half-frozen moss in the woods for table arrangements. I decided we needed an elaborate dessert display, so, as if we were back in Martha Stewart's cooking school, we made a spun sugar croquembouche, a bûche de Nöel, and a meringue buttercream Christmas tree cake that stood two feet high, along with dozens of Christmas cookies. We put up evergreens and decorated each room with a theme. When it was finished, holiday Blackberry looked spectacular.

That feature article put Blackberry on the map. People began coming not just from Nashville and around Tennessee, but from all over. We hired a chef, John Fleer, who updated our menu, and we added activities, like horseback riding and fly-fishing in Hesse Creek, the cold, clear stream that ran through Blackberry. When I wasn't driving back and forth between Alabama and Tennessee, I was working on Blackberry ideas.

At Rose Bay, I converted a children's playhouse into my office. That's where I was sitting when my phone rang and a PBS television producer from a fishing show said, "We want to do a story on a woman who fly-fishes. Do you fly-fish, Ms. Beall?" I thought for a second, and then, just as I had when Camille asked if anyone knew how to drive a boat, I gave a full-throated yes. I had never tied a fly or cast a line in my life.

We picked a production date and I hired a local angler in Mobile to teach me how to cast my line—standing on the blacktop in my driveway. No need to get my feet wet. Like learning how to shoot clays, I never thought about it. I learned how to bend my elbow and flick my wrist, but I thought it was all a bit unnecessary. Even though they said they wanted a woman, I was sure I could convince the producer to center the episode around my darling boys and Sandy, all three of whom knew how to fly-fish.

The host, the producer, and the crew arrived at Blackberry, and no matter how persuasive I thought I was going to be, they did in fact want a woman. I pulled on my waders, picked up my rod and reel, and walked into the waters of Hesse Creek. Just as I had been taught, I cocked my arm and released my wrist and elbow. I did it a few more times, until suddenly I felt a tug on my line. I stood absolutely frozen; it had never occurred to me to ask what to do if I actually caught a fish.

The fish, hooked and pulling on the long line, began swimming in circles around my waders. Slowly, the line began wrapping around my ankles, until I was as tangled and caught as the fish who had swallowed the fly.

Of course, the TV episode ran. And of course, I was still ready to follow my lifelong motto: saying that the answer is "yes," before I had even heard the question.

Chapter 13

GET OUT NOW

When Sam returned to Alabama, Sandy asked him, "So what did you learn from your year at boarding school?" Without missing a beat, Sam replied, "How good I have it at home."

Home was good. It was not simply that it was a beautiful house, although it was. I had embraced the Deep South's historic tradition of changing a home's décor to reflect the change of seasons, something I had learned in college when I worked as a tour guide at Gallier House in New Orleans. What's referred to as "Summer Dress" lightened a home and allowed the windows to be flung open to catch a breeze in the midst of stifling heat. Inside Rose Bay, the walls stayed the same linen white all year long, but in the winter, all the details were warm: there were Oriental rugs on the floors and traditional art hung on the walls. The chair fabric had patterns, accented with velvet pillows and velvet draperies on the windows. In the summer, white slipcovers shielded the furniture from the sun and heat, and the heavy velvet drapery was replaced with light linen drapes; I spread durable sisal rugs on the floor, impervious to sand, soil, and water, in place of the hot, wool Orientals. I even removed the antique books from the den—too likely to become musty—and replaced them with a collection of hat molds. I hung contemporary art on the walls, and then I opened the windows wide and didn't worry if bugs came in with the breeze. Everything from the off-season was stored in the attic. It was perfect for a Deep South house. Our house fit the seasons just as much as it fit our lives.

But Rose Bay was more than a house to us. It was probably the only component in our family's life that we all truly loved. Over the years, it evolved into a miniature, private Blackberry, a destination for both of our families. It was a place full of life, with something for everyone. Rose Bay was the one house that Sandy would never sell. He loved that house not simply because it was historic, but because he had an emotional connection to it. He had to get involved in the renovation, he had to give something of himself to get it finished, and in going to the job site, in watching it be transformed, Rose Bay had worked its way into his heart and soul, just as it had into mine.

Saturday, February 4, 1996, was a cold day, record cold for Lower Alabama with a nighttime low of eleven degrees. Sam was a freshman at Hampden-Sydney College in Virginia, and David was a senior in high school in Mobile, but was spending the night at a friend's house. Sandy and I had entertained all day. We had friends for lunch, family for dinner, and fires going in the fireplaces the entire time. After dinner, we might have finished a movie, but we went to bed early. About a quarter past eleven p.m., the alarm went off and the phone rang. I picked it up and heard the words "This is Hunter Security." Immediately,

I replied, "Everything's fine. Maybe the door blew open." "No, there's a fire," she said. Sandy jumped out of bed to search for the fire and I followed him. As we walked around outside, he spotted a thin skinny, red-hot line going up the side to the second story. It looked like a narrow wire of flame.

Sandy immediately grabbed the hose to attempt to put the fire out, but it didn't work. It was too cold—the connection wouldn't turn, and the water didn't come. Then I heard him yell, "Where are the fire extinguishers?" I answered, one downstairs and several upstairs in each of the bedrooms. He sprinted into the house and told me to call Hunter Security again and make sure the fire department knew where we were along the main road. I called Hunter, and the woman didn't even let me finish my question, instead she raised her voice and yelled, "Mrs. Beall, you'd better get out of the house!"

Sandy ran downstairs and said, "There is so much smoke I can't see anything." He could hardly breathe. I told him Hunter said to get out of the house. He asked if there was anything I wanted to grab. I thought for a second, and my mind didn't go to family photos or cherished mementos, I told Sandy, "I'm getting my Filofax; go get your laptop and your briefcase." We headed to the end of the driveway and waited for the firemen. There was no panic as we exited, me in my robe, clutching my calendar and address book and my wallet, Sandy holding his computer.

In that moment, I simply thought there would be a huge mess to clean up. I started thinking about the 172 sprinkler heads that were spread out around the property to water the lawn and the garden, and I worried that in the dark the fire trucks would probably run over the sprinkler heads and I'd have to get them fixed. I thought about what the water spraying from their hoses would do to the inside of the study and how the porch would probably be fine.

Sandy and I were partway down our long skinny driveway when we heard a bang. I turned. It was the sound of the upstairs windows being blown out by the fire. There were flames shooting out of the second story. When Sandy had gone upstairs and opened a couple of bedroom doors, he had inadvertently created an internal chimney. I heard the wail of sirens approaching, but it was too late. The only thing they could save were our neighbors' homes, and those only because, as I wrote two weeks later, "by the grace of God, the wind was blowing toward the bay."

Watching the flames, I buckled and collapsed on the driveway. I think it was a policeman who helped me into the old playhouse, which was now my office, and that's where we watched Rose Bay burn to the ground.

It took all of fifteen minutes to lose everything. Rose Bay was built with old lumber and lots of heart pine, which is heavy with resin and burns hotter and faster than other wood. The heat was so intense that the front ends of our cars melted. We couldn't move them because the keys were inside the burning house. We couldn't call anyone because the phone lines had burned, too, but people heard; neighbors must have called. Camille and Happy came. Our friends Lynn and Jimbo Meador came, followed by David and Joanne Cooper a few minutes later. David rushed back from his friend's house in Mobile. We just stood in silence, until David Cooper, who was chairman of the board of David's high school, UMS Wright, asked, "Are your books in the house?"

"No, sir," David said. "They're in my backpack in the car."

"Well," David Cooper told him, "go get them and throw them into the flames. You'll have an excuse forever." I do remember that we laughed.

As we stood, shivering and watching the smoke, embers, and ash, tears ran down my face. David put his arm around me and said, "Mom, you know what? It's just stuff. It's okay, Mom. It's just stuff." I tried to remember his words, spoken to comfort me, when Joanne, Camille, and their girls came to take me shopping the next afternoon because I had no clothes except for an ugly navy blazer that was at the dry cleaner's. I have tried to remember his words many times over the years.

When Sam found out what had happened, all he wanted to do was come home, even though there was no home left to come home to. There were no flights to Mobile because of bad weather, so Sam got in his car and started driving down from Virginia. He didn't get very far before his car hit a patch of ice and spun off the road and into a ditch. Sam walked away, but the car was totaled. He found a nearby house and I got a call from a woman who said, "Your son is on my front porch." I didn't want Sam to drive farther, so I called one of my parents' friends in Knoxville, who had a pilot's license, and asked if he would fly his small plane to get Sam and bring him home.

Rose Bay had been more than a house for Sam; it incubated his definition of and his passion for home. It was where he had introduced Sandy and me to Mary Celeste, the woman he would marry. Later, when he built his own house for his own family at Blackberry, he would incorporate much of Rose Bay's physical shape into the design. He duplicated the dining room, the porch, all of his favorite spaces, but even more, he replicated the heart that he felt in Rose Bay. He wanted a home with a table perpetually set for family and friends, where everyone would feel relaxed and welcome, where there was an atmosphere of warmth and belonging. That sense would become a touchstone for his life and vision, at work and at home.

Rose Bay was stuff, but it was, I came to realize much later, more than stuff. I did not mourn the rugs or the curtains or even the art. But I did grieve for the near-perfect life I had made there with my husband, boys, friends, and dogs. The flames couldn't take away the images of sweaty boys running inside for a snack after an afternoon of fishing, or the joy of gathering around the table with friends. Had our house not burned down, I am certain I would have stayed right where I was. And life would have been good. But in that moment, with that fire, the life we had built there also went up in flames and smoke.

In the aftermath, I told everyone I was fine. I put on a brave face for the outside world and willed things to be fine. I told anyone who asked that all that mattered was knowing my family was alive and safe, and I added, "For this I must thank God." Then in my next breath, I promised everyone, "We will rebuild, happier, stronger, and maybe even better." The only person who was doubtful was my new friend Suzanne Kasler, a prominent interior designer, who said, "I don't understand how you talk about that house. You're too nonchalant. You're not dealing with it." I waved her off, but she was right. I wasn't. Years later, Sandy would say, "I am very good, fortunately or unfortunately, at not dwelling on the past." But even he still cries over Rose Bay.

Almost twenty years later, Sam and I would sit in a psychologist's office and he would tell me about the mother he remembered from Rose Bay and how much he wanted her back. But none of us could go back. Try as I might, something vital was lost with that house and could not be recovered. I could not become that woman again. Rose Bay was my first lesson that not even a gilded cage is fireproof. And what is lost is not simply the cage, but the beautiful birds inside.

Chapter 14

GOOD, BETTER, BEST

Sandy and I moved into Rose Bay's guesthouse and started making plans to rebuild. We hired architects, and traveled to Beaufort, South Carolina, to look at antebellum homes and contemplate a different design. Where Rose Bay had stood I planted towering sunflowers and an array of other blooming flowers and vegetables. I called it the Phoenix Garden, because I believed that on this spot a new house would rise. Then one early-August morning, as I stood outside on the tiny guesthouse porch, drinking my steaming hot coffee and watching the water in the bay, I heard a voice say to me, "Do not rebuild. It's time to move."

I called Sandy. He was away, as he so often was during the week, traveling for business. I called his hotel room and told him, "I don't think we need to rebuild. I think we need to move." He never said yes or no—he simply asked, "Where?" and I answered, "Atlanta." His next words were "Meet me there." By Sunday, we had found a townhouse.

Our move to Atlanta coincided with a frenzied period of

building at Blackberry. We added a group of ten cottages that I named Holly Glade, as well as a stone and wood house for Sandy and me, which I named Maple Cottage. I buried my emotions in work and insulated my wounds, priming us all to look forward, not back. Periodically, I would think, *What if we had rebuilt in Point Clear?* But as much as I loved Rose Bay, something in me knew that we could not have stayed. Nothing would have been what it was.

Our time in Atlanta was short-lived. As it turned out, Ruby Tuesday was on the move as well. After looking at Charlotte, Atlanta, metro Washington, D.C., and Knoxville, the executive team chose Knoxville in part because of the company's roots. Then Knoxville and the adjoining town of Maryville began competing, and Maryville made a better offer. Ruby Tuesday's team wanted to be part of the community Maryville offered. With the company's move from Mobile to Maryville, the cutting of the cord with our prior life was nearly complete. We drew up plans to build the RT (short for Ruby Tuesday) Lodge at Blackberry. We were going home.

I read once that sunrise and sunset are not miracles, because they are expected, but rainbows are miracles because they are not. That was a bit like how it felt to have Blackberry and Ruby Tuesday suddenly be fourteen miles apart. Then Sam and Mary Celeste announced they had both decided to transfer to the University of Tennessee to finish their degrees, and they would live at Blackberry. It felt like we were rebuilding our family. As Dr. J. Vernon McGee wrote, God "makes great doors swing on little hinges."

Rose Bay was to be the site of one last Beall memory. On August 30, 1997, the same day as Sandy's and my anniversary, at sunset, Sam married Mary Celeste. Sandy and I had offered to host, and I arranged everything long distance, with Camille's help, because at the same time I was installing sixteen guest bedrooms to be ready for a guest's wedding at Blackberry that same weekend. It was no big deal for me to install all those rooms and then turn around and drive to Alabama and help host an enormous wedding. I was all about the sprint and the finish, not pausing to catch my breath.

The wedding was held in the old clapboard Sacred Heart Catholic chapel that overlooks the water. We had the reception underneath a huge tent where our house used to be, with lights strung among the trees. Even at dusk, it was the hottest wedding that ever existed, with no air-conditioning in the church and no air-conditioning outside. But that magical night was healing in so many ways. Sam and Mary Celeste had made our final "homecoming" a joyous one. Instead of the harsh light of flames, we would remember the soft, easy glow of lanterns. The last sounds we shared were of laughter, music, and dancing. The memories being made were of lives joining together and a new home beginning. My eyes welled up as I watched my little boy, once most likely to hold a Ping-Pong paddle or a fishing pole, now tenderly take his new bride's hand. In Mary Celeste, Sam had found someone who loved and cherished home as much as he did. She never hesitated for a second when he said he wanted to celebrate outside on the grass at Rose Bay. She never hesitated whenever he burst in with a new idea, a new passion, or a new dream. They were so young when they spoke their vows, but when it came to the part about "to love and to cherish," they understood the depth of the words, the pledge to each other of "yes," and all that would mean.

After Sam's wedding, we sold Rose Bay. It was time. The family that bought it never rebuilt the main house. They lived in the guesthouse. The only way anyone would ever know that another house existed was if they noticed a redbrick walkway that came up from the boardwalk and suddenly dead-ended in the middle of a bright green lawn.

Sometimes I would think, *God burned my house down and He did it for a reason.* I was certain that the reason was to send me back to my true home. I never thought He wanted me to sit and think about what a home is and what makes a house a home. I thought I was simply meant to keep replicating the same life I had made before, just bigger and at Blackberry.

In 1990, for our first Christmas where Blackberry was open to outside guests, I had visited the gift shop at the Museum of Appalachia. I wanted to have local gifts for each guest, gifts that would be wrapped and placed in the tiny stockings hung on their doorknobs. One of the toys I found was a long, skinny paddle with three holes, a rubber band for the sides, and a ball attached. The game was simple: try to get the ball in the "best" hole. The holes were named Good, Better, and Best, and on the underside was the quote

---

"Good, better, best, never let it rest,
'til the good is better and the better is best."

That became my new motto. I wanted every little thing at Blackberry to progress from good to better to best: best service, best food, best arrival, best beds, best linens. Once I was doing an interview alongside our manager, Matt Alexander, and the writer asked, "What's the best thing and what's the worst thing about Blackberry?" Matt pointed to me and said, "She is." And it was true: I was always changing something, trying to make it better or best. I wanted it to be not only the best place to stay, but the best place to work, the best experience possible. (I didn't know then that quote "good, better, best" had in fact nothing to do with the world of things. It was written by Saint Jerome, who lived about A.D. 420 and was focused on living a Christian, moral life.)

Food had always been a centerpiece of the Blackberry experience, so I decided to take that a step further and incorporate a cooking school. I wanted guests to have the same exciting "aha, I can do this" moment that I had at Kathleen Barron's and Martha Stewart's. I wanted them to feel that they could make the same magic in their own kitchen and then enjoy sitting down to eat it, to see everything from prep chopping to table-setting tricks and then to go home inspired. Our guests were as interested in cooking as I was. It didn't take long before we had twenty-four Blackberry guests in and out of our Maple Cottage house on Monday and Tuesday, the cooking school days, and a rotation of tables in the dining space and out on the porch.

Running a cooking school that looks effortless takes a significant amount of work. There wasn't a large, unused kitchen just sitting around at Blackberry, which is why I set up the school at my home. I hired Thresia Moneymaker, who had worked at Blackberry, to help me. Thresia and I would set the tables with silver, crystal, and china; do the floral centerpieces, always using at least a few roses, which had become my signature, and adding in whatever else might be fresh—hydrangeas, branches, greenery; and then disappear out the door to let Chef John Fleer or another guest chef teach. Then we'd come back to clean up once everyone had gone.

Having no boundary between work and home was what I had done when we started Blackberry. It was easy to reorder our lives to repeat that familiar pattern, living and working in the the same space. Busyness also provided me with a kind of numbing comfort. I didn't have to dwell on what had been lost, I didn't have to think too hard about the trauma of the fire, losing our home, escaping with our lives. Every time I closed the door of the Maple Cottage, I believed that we were safe.

THE SEASONS OF A HOME

———

Many of us, even in warm-weather climates, increasingly refresh our homes according to the season—plants and light colors for spring, decorated decks and porches for summer, deeper, heavier colors for fall, an abundance of throws, pillows, and candles for winter.

But our homes also reflect the seasons of our life. I remember my first apartment on Fern Street in New Orleans. My mom decorated it in "shabby chic" slipcovers with beautiful throws, pillows, and sisal carpeting. Small homes make the most of a few things: light, expectant, hopeful. Those homes reflect the time when we are planting seeds and starting to grow.

My "summer" season house was Blackberry Farm, where, with my husband and children, I put down my roots of home. Everything was full.

Fall was Rose Bay, the harvest after a long growing season. So much bounty everywhere I looked. Sandy and I would sit on the big porch overlooking the bay and feel the cooling breeze rush in off the water, or on chilly nights, eat in the study in front of the fire. Nearly everything important we had accumulated in twenty years together was stored there.

The winter home follows when your children are grown and you live your lives as mature adults, either with your spouse or with yourself.

But like the calendar and the seasons, winter is never the end. Spring always follows with a fresh season of renewal. For me, it has become a season with my grandchildren and the "spring" of my spiritual life, watching the first buds and blossoms of my re-lationship with God. Home can heal; it can restore.

Living through all the seasons of a home is important—renovations are often best after you have lived in a space for a full cycle. So, too, with our lives: we need to spend four seasons with someone to reach the next level of a relationship, to truly know them. Spring is always giddy, but waiting through winter gives you the opportunity to see whether your ties have frozen in place or whether something new will grow.

Chapter 15

HUMPTY DUMPTY
HAD A GREAT FALL

It's funny what you remember when you can't remember much of anything. On Sunday afternoon, November 14, 1999, Sandy was in Louisiana for the opening day of duck hunting season and I was getting ready to fly to London to visit friends. Sam and Mary Celeste had offered to take me to the airport after I finished my luncheon meeting about fly-fishing. By then, we had been living at Blackberry for nearly a year, and it was not uncommon for me to work seven days a week.

Here's what I remember: I left the lunch and drove down the big hill in a golf cart. (Golf carts were and still are how everyone gets around at Blackberry.) I remember Sam pulling up to the Maple Cottage in his Ford Bronco to get my luggage. I remember we talked about stopping on the way to the airport to look at a piece of property in Maryville where he might want to settle with Mary Celeste and their daughter, Cameron, after he finished culinary school and an apprenticeship in California. I remember him leaving to pick up Mary Celeste and Cameron at their farmhouse, just around the bend in the road, so the four of us could ride together, and that he was coming back to collect me. All that was left to do was for me to gather a few remaining things. That is my last real memory. After that my mind is blank, until the moment I woke up in the ICU.

In between those two points in time, all I have are other people's recollections. What they know is that I fell in the driveway, and my head smacked a sharp edge of the cut granite curb. There was no blood, but I was knocked unconscious. Sam held me and tried to wake me, cradling my head in his hands. Eventually I came to and after several minutes attempted to sit up, but I kept repeating over and over again, "Something's not right, something's not right." A clear fluid had begun to drip out of my nose. It wasn't mucus. It was brain matter. Sam kept holding me as he shouted to Mary Celeste to call an ambulance.

Thresia, my housekeeper, remembers how minutes after, as soon as she ran out the door she saw sheets of paper strewn all over the ground and a stray pair of pantyhose. She remembers staring at the slick leather soles of my boots and thinking how smooth they were, not practical for walking and impossible to get any traction. She remembers seeing me lying on the ground, Sam cradling my head and yelling for Mary Celeste as I tried to sit up. She remembers how after the ambulance left, my little granddaughter Cameron looked at the tire mark ground deep into the grass and wagged her finger, shook her head from side to side, and said, "Yaya." Yaya was her name for me, and what Cameron was saying was that Yaya would not approve of that tire messing up her pristine lawn.

Reverend Doug Banister remembers walking the grounds at Blackberry. He wasn't usually there on Sundays, but my neighbor, Dee, and her husband had invited him. He remembers hearing the wail of the siren and following the sound to the edge of the Maple Cottage. Doug came to the hospital to pray over me, even though we had never met.

The EMTs didn't bother with the closest hospital in Maryville. Instead I was rushed to the emergency room at the University of Tennessee Hospital in Knoxville. In the ER, scans showed my brain was bleeding. The hospital phoned one of its top neuro-surgeons, Dr. Bill Reid, who raced over.

For the first twenty-eight hours, the doctors decided the best course was watchful waiting. I was hooked up to all kinds of tubes and machines. When Sandy saw me, he remembers simply feeling utter "sadness." The bleeding didn't stop, and my brain started to swell. I was rushed to the operating room and Dr. Reid attempted to place a shunt into my head to siphon off the excess blood. The shunt didn't work. Dr. Reid came out of the OR and told Sandy, "You have a choice to make: gamble that the bleeding will stop, or open her head up and create some room for her brain to prevent more damage." Opening up my head meant removing a portion of my skull. As Sandy put it, "We aren't going to gamble with Kreis." There was no time for me to fear the scalpel, the microfine drill, or the scrubs. I was already in a medically induced coma. There was, though, plenty of time for Sandy and the rest of my family to be terrified. My craniotomy lasted for hours.

When I eventually woke up, I did not know that I was in the ICU or how many days had passed: I wasn't lucid enough to panic or even wonder why I was lying in a bed. I turned my head slowly to the left and made out Sam's face and his piercing blue eyes. He took my hand and simply said, "Mom, you had an accident. You are in the hospital. You are going to be okay."

The next day he told me, "I am the reason you are in the hospital." I had fallen because somehow I had collided with or had tried to avoid his SUV. Or had just been startled by the sound and lost my footing. No one could ever be certain because no one saw anything until after I was on the ground. But, as with other things, Sam took it upon himself to shoulder the burden.

We were not an affectionate family, outside of all those months baby David was carried around, but I remember Sam touching me, his hand lightly stroking my hand or my arm as he spoke. It is one of my strongest memories after the accident but it would have stood out anyway because it was very rare for Sam to hug, let alone have his hand on mine.

I, of course, didn't remember what had happened, would never remember what had happened, and I didn't want to know the details. It was an accident. Like all accidents, there is some measure of second-guessing, but in my case, never blame. The truth is, none of us will ever know. And that's okay. Here my inclination for relentless forward momentum was a blessing. It ensured that I never looked back or asked "Why me?"

Time restarted when I opened my eyes in the ICU and saw my family standing around me. Sandy was my protector and advocate, arriving before dawn to talk to the medical team when they made their rounds, the proverbial "squeaky wheel." Despite all those hours of surgery, I was never in pain. I probably should have felt alarm or maybe fear, but I didn't feel anything. I was simply still, staring out into the controlled chaos that surrounded me. All I heard was everyone saying over and over again that everything was "okay."

The top half of my head was shaved, and I had staples running across my skull from ear to ear like a set of railroad tracks. Yet thanks to a constant infusion of good drugs and Sam's heroic removal of the mirror in the intensive care bathroom, I wasn't even aware of that. Sam knew how vain his mom was and still is. If I had seen what I really looked like, that revelation would have terrified me more than my injuries. I still have no idea how Sam snuck in with a set of tools, unscrewed the mirror from the wall, and hauled it out, but I will always be grateful that he did.

I stayed in the ICU for more than a week, drifting in and out of sleep, while my medical team decided what to do with me. Of course, it was a miracle that I had woken up, but I could barely stand and could not manage more than a few halting steps at a time. Somewhere along the way, I had also lost my sense of smell, much of my ability to taste, and about seventy percent of my hearing, but I didn't realize it then.

The doctors recommended that I go to the neurological recovery floor at the Fort Sanders Regional Medical Center to continue healing. But Sandy, bless his stubborn heart, refused. The medical team had known me for all of ten days. Sandy had known me nearly twenty-five years. The man who was CEO of hundreds of Ruby Tuesday restaurants by then was determined to be CEO of my care. He told them, "No, Kreis loves home and that's where I'm taking her."

No gift, past or present, has ever matched those words. My home was where I needed to be. Taking me home was the kindest, nicest thing anyone could have done. Sandy moved his office into the house; I remember lying in bed in our first-floor bedroom and watching men trying to get Sandy's computer seamlessly connected with his office in Maryville. He took care of me around the clock, making sure I got the vital anti-seizure medicine, which I dreaded and often refused to take—it was a battle of wills several times a day. He knew I would be a head-strong patient and knew he had to be there.

On the way home from the hospital, I decided I was going to join everyone for Thanksgiving dinner the next afternoon. I had planned the menu and table decorations and organized the guest list weeks before my accident. Of course, I knew I couldn't cook it and arrange it, but I convinced myself that I was going to sit at the table. Instead, it was all I could do to sit up in bed. My family and guests quickly trooped through the bedroom, while I sat, propped up with pillows, as if I had the flu. Off in the dining room, conversation went on, silverware clinked, water and wine gurgled as they were poured into glasses, but my newly deaf ears heard none of it. My door was closed, and I was alone on the other side. The accident was very much like that, a door that I had walked through and slammed shut behind me, leaving me stuck in my own room and there was no going back to the other side.

I was largely immobile for the first several weeks. My brain was very fragile. It was too taxing to do almost any thinking or processing at all, which meant no books or television. On what I would call my "happy slug drugs," I was able to manage two things, either lie in my bed or curl up by the fireplace.

As soon as I was able, Sandy took me on daily walks on the closest path at Blackberry, although "walking" is a generous term. It was more like shuffling and scuffling. I put on my full-length brown coat and gripped a black enamel cane to steady myself while Sandy held my other arm. Despite Sam's best ef-forts, I did eventually see myself in a mirror. I looked like the

Beverly Hillbillies version of Frankenstein's monster with my mullet and staples. My answer was to wear elegant scarves to cover my gruesome head.

This was, I believed, all temporary. I never envisioned anything less than a perfect outcome. But the brain is a mysterious storehouse for everything that makes us uniquely ourselves. When it is jostled around the way mine was, the consequences aren't always immediately clear.

Walking was something I could will myself to do and was slowly working my way back to, but the fall had also completely severed a nerve connected to my hearing. I didn't immediately realize the extent of the damage. Maybe it was the drugs, maybe it was being tucked in the quiet of our bedroom and only going for short walks with Sandy or having Thresia come and fuss over me, but it took me a little while to process the absence of sound.

I didn't hear birds or cars or the vacuum. I didn't hear what people said if they weren't standing in front of me and looking into my face. Sandy could raise his voice and make a comment from another room or the hallway and nothing registered. It was as if I were scuba diving, as I had done during my college years, dropping into a silent world where the only clear sound was the whoosh of the breathing regulator attached to my mouth. But this time I was never going to surface, never going to break the plane into a world where I could simultaneously hear the slap of the ocean, the sound of the outboard motor, the creaking of the boat deck, and another human voice—and recognize each one as distinct and true. My new reality was that I was going to be a mostly deaf person in a hearing world. What I was still trying to grapple with was the realization that no one else would notice unless I told them. When Camille came to see me, the first thing I asked her was "Do I look like I can't hear?"

It was the same with my senses of smell and taste. No matter how much I tried, I was always going to be unable to savor the scents of my garden or the aroma of a meal. One of the first things I noticed was that I had no appetite. The only food I craved was cream cheese and olive sandwiches with mayonnaise, my mother's favorite meal when I was little. Something about the briny taste of the olives, the different textures, and the memories resonated with my now muted taste buds.

For a long time after the accident, I thought that if I could make the outside of me look normal, the inside would somehow follow. I was determined to make my accident simply a bump in the road, or in my case, on my head. Holed up in the comfort of my bed, I could pull up the covers and push away any problems. After all, I told myself, I had a caring, attentive husband and a beautiful home to get well in. Whether it was the drugs or my perpetual optimism, I truly thought everything would go back to the way it had been before that November afternoon. I never considered the alternative.

My medical team was focused on healing my brain. I had a prescription to go to the Patricia Neal Center, named for the famous Tennessee actress who had suffered a stroke, for rehabilitation therapy. Thresia drove me each way. It took me eighteen years to learn that she had never driven on the big four-lane Alcoa highway before we made those trips. She had practiced the route for days with her husband riding in the passenger seat to learn how to merge into the traffic and memorize which exit to take, all because she hadn't wanted to say no when I asked her to take me.

I went to Patricia Neal twice. Watching the stroke victims, the car accident victims, the people who couldn't feed themselves, who were struggling to walk or to talk, was overwhelming. I also felt as if I didn't belong. My needs were very different. On the outside, I looked fine. I could walk, I could feed myself, I could carry on a basic conversation. I did not look like I was struggling. All the damage was on the inside. But I couldn't explain that, and I also didn't know how to get my brain to heal on my own.

I felt as if I should be able to do everything that I had done before the accident. Yet when I tried, my mind was quickly overwhelmed by fatigue. Worse still, I was terrible at slowing down, let alone resting. I hadn't really taken any time off from work since I was twenty-three. I lived my life by lists and tasks and I measured my worth on the basis of my completion rates. After Rose Bay burned down, Sandy and I went on a building bender of expansions and improvements. Since we moved back to Tennessee, I had spent my days with Blackberry-hired contractors and designers, with Blackberry's chief gardener, with our executive chef, our manager, and the people who worked in operations. With very few exceptions, Blackberry paid the salaries of every one of my friends. Blackberry was my whole world.

As much as I did not fit at Patricia Neal, now I no longer fit at Blackberry.

My biggest setback after the accident came when I tried to return to the most rudimentary part of my Blackberry self.

A few years before as we expanded, I had started a program called Room Quest. It happened every January, although that year I started a bit late. Room Quest was simple: I would go around to each guest room and cottage and make what was essentially a punch list of everything that needed to be repaired or redone—paint, patch, fix a plug, replace a carpet, new drapery, new pillows, new lamps. It had always been a very straightforward and satisfying task.

In February my young assistant named Teresa (whom I nick-named T to separate her from my housekeeper, Thresia) and I set off on a golf cart to do our inventory and make lists with specific categories, items, and numbers. That little bit of pro-cessing set me back for about three weeks. At first, I tried sitting in my bed, looking at the lists. My brain fogged over, and I felt as disconnected as I had following the accident. Like a cold I couldn't shake, the grogginess lingered. My mind was tired and no amount of sleep or quiet could refresh it. What was worse was the realization that one simple task had so utterly defeated me. I had gone from being a marathon processor and doer who could work for hours and never tire to suddenly becoming ex-hausted from thinking about something as small and familiar as a basic punch list. For the first time, I couldn't fall back on my easy mottos and motivating clichés.

As part of my New Year's resolutions, I had made a list, and one of the things on my list was to find a neuropsychologist who could tell me what I could and couldn't do with this injury. But that had proven to be another dead end. The Knoxville psychologist I was referred to hadn't bothered to read my medi-cal report. Instead, he spent most of our hour asking me about my childhood and my relationship with my parents, as if he were following his own checklist straight from Sigmund Freud. I came home frustrated, and just as he had done in the ICU, Sandy took charge. He said, "We're going to the Shepherd Cen-ter in Atlanta." The Shepherd Center had been started by the parents of James Shepherd, who had suffered a serious spinal cord injury when he was twenty-two. James Shepherd was the same age as Sandy, and the three of us had met at a business conference. When James was injured, there were few rehabilita-tion and care options for spinal and brain injuries in the south-eastern U.S., so his family set out to change that. Sandy got me two appointments with a neuropsychologist named Dr. Stephen Macciocchi. My mind was still so scrambled at that point that I couldn't even process the combination of three new sounds and syllables—I was never able to properly pronounce his name.

Dr. Macciocchi read my medical file. He showed me the small bump that was now a permanent feature of my forehead and explained that when I hit my head, my brain had been jarred forward. The frontal lobe had smashed into my skull. He called it a "shocking blow." The clarity of his explanation was reassuring. Then came the prescription. He told me that the only way to heal from this injury was to do nothing: no working, no reading, no thinking. I could do other things, he said, but not processing. I could not, he explained, do anything that would require my mind to work too hard. My brain was like a broken leg, and in order for it to heal properly, I needed to stay off it. But what did it mean to "stay off your brain"? With a broken leg, walking too soon causes pain and setbacks, but a brain injury is different. There was no pain, I couldn't look at an X-ray and be told where it was healing and how far it had to go. How much would be too much? I wondered.

I never verbalized any of these concerns to Dr. Macciocchi or to Sandy. Instead, I went to my two appointments, then returned to Blackberry, where everyone I knew was someone who worked with Sandy and me. All of them were nice, just as they had always been. They never treated me differently, but I knew the one person in the group or in the conversation who didn't "work right" was me.

Whenever Sandy and I had been faced with a major life event, good or bad, it had always led to a building project. Sam's impending birth happened simultaneously with us acquiring Blackberry Farm, the disruption of the boys going to boarding school led to the renovation of Rose Bay, the fire at Rose Bay led to moving back to Tennessee and an expansion at Blackberry. I'm not sure if building redirected our excess energy or if it gave us something to accomplish together, but it was the balm we applied to whatever ailed us. The accident proved no different. In those early months, Sandy found another house for us. It was located in Knoxville on Kenesaw Avenue, the same street where I had grown up as a child, and it needed a complete redo. I named it the Pretty Woman house, after the Julia Roberts movie. Like Julia's character when she shops in Beverly Hills, I couldn't do it myself and so I learned how to sit back and let people come to me.

Sandy hired the team we had used at Blackberry, Hickory Construction, led by Chuck Alexander, and the Spitzmiller and Norris architectural firm, and I asked for Suzanne Kasler to design the interiors. This was to be my rehab, to be surrounded by people who spoke my language of building, design, and visuals. I sat in my favorite chair and looked at what they showed me. We traveled together to shop, but since I was the client, once I made my picks, I didn't have to follow through. Someone else would make sure that the choices were carried out. Each person on the project was patient and kind, each a person I could trust. I was able to let go and have faith in the strength of our relationships.

Suzanne walked into my life at exactly the right time. On the interiors, she was never dismissive; she was encouraging without being overwhelming, and boy, did I need that. Working on the Pretty Woman house was healing. For eight months, it was my primary focus. I was part of something without having to do the heavy work. Building is my drug, and this house was a great tranquilizer to make me feel good. Taking those baby steps was how I thought I was going to get my life back.

The basics of life did slowly return. In the early spring, the Patricia Neal Center called me to ask if I wanted to take a driving course. I feigned being out of town, but in fact, I had already been driving for two weeks. I had found it very hard to drive my SUV, so Sandy got me a sedan. The one maneuver I hated was backing up. There was something unsettling about it, not just from a spatial, processing perspective, but deeper. I suppose I was afraid of going backward.

By August, I was well enough to make that long-postponed trip to London to visit my friends. I even bought a book in the airport, *Angela's Ashes,* which was in many ways a terrible choice for someone pushing through the darkness of a major brain trauma, but I was grateful to be able to read on the plane rather than just watch a movie. Taking that trip, holding a book in my hand, I finally felt as if I was coming back.

That fall, we moved into the Kenesaw house, but despite the progress I was making, I have only spotty memories of that time. Sandy and I threw a huge Christmas party, we were on the Knoxville Museum of the Arts Christmas home tour, and *Southern Accents* came to do an extensive photoshoot for a feature on the house and Suzanne. Little Cameron came back from California to stay with us. I remember her playing in the playroom we had added downstairs. But that is all I have. On the details of everyday life, my mind draws a blank.

I was no longer partially bald. I stopped wearing scarves to cover my head and cut my old and new hair short. As my hair grew back, I discovered I could no longer wear ponytails, after the crainiotomy pulling my thick hair back and wraping it in an elastic hurt. Time also fixed the shuffle in my walk. To the outside world I looked like a woman of relative leisure, with a house in town and a house at Blackberry. I even dipped my toe back into Blackberry design and did the interiors for two houses.

Then, too, I didn't know how to look anything but successful. I didn't know how to be approachable outside of work, and the people I knew were uncertain about how to approach me. I knew something was the matter, but I couldn't articulate it. So, each day I put on the same mask and said everything was fine, while inside I was a wounded person who wouldn't admit to the wound. Worse, I wasn't sure what the wound was.

Neither Sandy nor I had ever had to ask for sustained help before. More specifically, I didn't know how to ask. Growing up, I had never asked for help from my parents. Within our own families, Sandy and I were the ones who took care of other people, opening our guest rooms, consulting on jobs, paying for events, schooling, trips to a psychologist. I didn't know how to reach out to Sandy, or to our families, or to my small group of genuine friends like Camille. In Knoxville, I only knew an assortment of high school acquaintances, most of whom I hadn't seen in more than twenty years. I couldn't—or didn't—call and say, "Hey, I've had an accident and I need a friend."

When you are the fixers, the people around you don't necessarily think that there might come a time when you need fixing.

I wanted life to be exactly what it had been before the accident. But it couldn't be, because I wasn't the same. Instead I replayed the same loop: *Act the same, look the same, be the same, you are the same.* That became my new mantra.

The truth, however, was that nothing was ever going to be the same again.

Chapter 16

WHAT'S WRONG
WITH THIS PICTURE?

Sometime after the accident, Doug Banister and his wife, co-incidentally enough named Sandi, came to dinner with Sandy and me. During the meal, we carried on a nice conversation about nothing that I can remember, then at the end of the evening, as we stood in the front hallway and said our goodbyes, Doug asked if he could pray with me. I said yes, and Doug put his hands on my shoulders and began speaking to God.

I wish I could say that I felt some jolt of transformation or powerful embrace of healing, but there was nothing like that. Then, too, I'm more of a hit-me-square-in-the-face type of person, and even that apparently doesn't really work. After all, I'm the one who arrived at Blackberry and immediately went inside to look at the kitchen and the rooms, largely ignoring how the house was perched on the top of a hill, the peaks of the Smokies cresting just beyond. It took a while for me to even notice how removing the scrubby overgrowth and some untrimmed trees would open up a lovely view. In retrospect, there's no reason to think my path to faith would be any different.

Sandy and I did go to Doug's church. It was completely unlike the Presbyterian churches I knew, where the Sunday service ran like clockwork and next to nothing had changed in the last fifty years. At Doug's church, there were no Bibles, no traditional hymns, just big screens and contemporary music. Baptisms were a centerpiece event with full immersion up on the big stage, rather than a discreet sprinkling of water on the back of the head. But what truly set it apart was the sermon. It was mesmerizing. I had never heard a speaker like Doug. Yet, I think Sandy and I attended services maybe three or four times. Sandy briefly joined Doug's men's Bible study, and then we stopped. We didn't stick with things like that. We stuck with work.

The accident, however, was testing that system. A year passed, and I still wasn't working full-time and didn't want to. Fortuitously, two months before I hit my head, we had hired Matt Alexander to be our general manager, and he had temporarily assumed many of my duties and was doing a great job. Blackberry was a family business and we had always planned on passing it to our children, and the son who was most interested was Sam. He was set to return to Blackberry in 2002, so I knew we would have a pair of good hands and a passionate heart ready to lead.

For 2001, I set a goal of restoring my physical health, believing if I did that, the rest of life would follow. I started walking around Knoxville and hiking at Blackberry, and when I felt ready, I visited the Ashram in California, a holistic retreat that offered hiking, yoga, and meditation, as well as a fresh vegan diet. I had gone there with Camille in 1999. It was the last trip

I had taken before my injury. When at the end of a grueling morning hike I once again stood on top of the Santa Monica mountains, looking out at the desert landscape, feeling my legs burn and the breath stab in my lungs, I felt like planting a victory flag.

I had triumphed over the physical part of my injury. But the mental and emotional parts of my life still refused to get into gear.

I tried to send my brain on the physical equivalent of an Ashram hike, signing myself up for design school in Atlanta four days a week, heading out from Blackberry on Sunday night and returning on Thursday. I registered for a University of Tennessee extension course on beekeeping. But what finally spoke to me was a list of twelve great things to try in 2002 in the glossy, thick stock pages of *Town & Country* magazine. Of course, I am a sucker for lists: punch lists, shopping lists, checklists. One item on that list was an intensive, eleven-week course that summer at the Rocky Mountain School of Photography. I thought, *I like taking pictures. I could become a photographer.* That was about as introspective as I got.

The school was in Missoula, Montana, and I asked Keith to take the course with me. At first, she didn't want to. She said, "I don't know anything about photography and you know too much." But I told her all I knew was how to put my camera on program and press the green shutter button, so she agreed.

I truly don't know why I asked her. The longest stretch of time we had spent living in the same space had been two decades ago in Hilton Head. She had been numbingly inebriated or slightly hungover for most of it, and I had been completely besotted with running a restaurant, which made me equally oblivious. We were not confidantes or confessional talkers.

Keith would have described us both as adhering to the "shovel your own damn stall" school of sisterhood. The last time we had been affectionately close was probably Halloween when I was five years old. My mother made me an angel costume, with light gossamer wings, while Keith dressed up as a cowboy. When it came time to trick or treat, it had started to drizzle, and neither of our parents wanted to go out in the rain. So the damp cowboy and the watery angel trudged up and down the hill by ourselves with our sacks, holding hands.

Yet somehow I was struck with the overwhelming urge to go to Montana with my big sister, without the buffer of four children, my husband, her boyfriend, and work, and she said yes.

Keith drove by herself, with her new Welsh terrier. She mapped out the northern cross-country route and listened to books on tape. I had made sure that the condo was furnished and all the drawers were labeled, furnishings arranged, beds made, towels hung in the bathrooms, and the key left waiting over the door. Keith was thrilled. She is even more compulsively organized than I am. It shocked her to see how much we are alike.

We had a full kitchen, but we never cooked. Keith was on a fitness kick, which began with a breakfast shake that we shared, followed by Wendy's taco salad for lunch, and going out to dinner, because class ended at six and we knew we had a health shake awaiting us in the morning. In eleven weeks, we didn't deviate, except for the case of blueberries we ate making the five-hour drive to the edge of Yellowstone to sleep in a B&B where we had to share a double bed and a bathroom.

When the summer intensive started, we had been assigned to different groups, but Keith marched up to the organizer and told him to put us in the same group, saying she hadn't come all this way to be separated from her sister. The girl who wouldn't eat her peas wouldn't swallow this, while I had accepted the list as final and the placements done.

At forty-eight and fifty, we were by far the oldest people there. Once a week for an hour, we had a lesson on the basics of digital photography. The instructor had everyone break into two-person teams and gave each team a red Solo cup. If there was a question, the red cup was supposed to be placed on the top of the computer monitor as a signal that the team needed help. For the entire hour, Keith and I never took our red cup down.

We went to the darkroom together, went to rodeos, went to see *My Big Fat Greek Wedding* in the little downtown theater, ran around the condo grounds when her dog got loose. All those years that I had tended my roses, packed up on weekends, and spread my quilts on picnic tables, gone on building benders . . . what if I had tried to seed and water a relationship with my sister? But maybe we couldn't have done it before then; maybe we needed to let our childhoods and early adulthoods lie fallow for a couple of decades. Or maybe at long last we were ready to start growing up.

Without knowing it, Keith and I were studying photography in the twilight years of film, just before digital images took over. This meant we learned how to print in a darkroom. I loved the hours spent watching the images slowly materialize on the paper, trying different techniques to capture just the right light. I also loved the silence. In the darkroom, the only thing I needed were my eyes, not my damaged ears.

The summer intensive had taught me that I loved making close-up images of plants and also portraits, and I left thinking I would start a photography business in Knoxville. I also persuaded Keith to move back to Tennessee. She found a house a short drive away from mine and started a new career, breeding Welsh terriers. (In 2017, one of her dogs was named the top terrier in the nation.)

It is too much to say that after eleven weeks, our relationship was completely transformed. It was more that for the first time we *had* a relationship, one unmediated by the gravitational pull of our parents and the orbiting moons of our children. Had Keith drunk herself to death or overdosed or had I ended up incapacitated after my fall, we never would have met each other. Relationships, I learned that summer, could be renovated, but it was a slow, meandering job that could not be rushed.

Back in Knoxville, I made lists of to-dos to begin a photography business. Then Sandy announced he wanted us to move back to Blackberry full time. This time I spoke up, asking him, "Are you sure?" I thought it would be too easy for us, particularly me, to become caught up in the work side of Blackberry again. I thought Sam and Mary Celeste might need their own space. It wasn't long, however, before I had my answer. Within months, we had sold the Pretty Woman house and were back living in the Maple Cottage.

But like any two parties in a long-term relationship, Blackberry had changed, and I knew that I had changed, too.

In our absence, Maple Cottage had become very much part of the day-to-day operations at Blackberry. Now I felt like the one intruding on the needs of Blackberry and its guests. There were golf carts and vehicles lined up in the driveway for cooking schools. I was always careful to enter through a side door so as not to disturb anything. And at night, when I went into my kitchen, more often than not, I had to search for what I wanted. Utensils, glasses, pots and pans, nothing was put back in the same place—and this for the woman who labeled drawers for a three-month condo rental.

Sandy's experience was completely different. He would leave for work and the house looked fine; he would come home eight hours later and never be aware of what had happened while he was gone. But I felt too much like an interloper. I loved Blackberry, but it had been freeing to be away and do something totally different—it had given both Blackberry and me a chance to evolve. What I failed to appreciate, though, was how deeply these changes had also changed the overall dynamic of our family.

Blackberry began as my partnership with Sandy, it was the business-child we raised together. Like a mother, I had never received a paycheck. I always told Sandy, "Just put any money I might make back into the business." Instead, my fulfillment came from the decision making and the doing, from having a vision and seeing it realized.

After the accident, I knew it was the right thing for Sam to take over the lead role. Yes, he was twenty-six, but I had been all of twenty-three when we bought the property and opened the inn. We had a great staff that had been working with us for years and were loyal to the place and to our family. Plus, Sam had professional training. It is deeply gratifying to know that your child wants the business you have built. But when I stepped away and Sam stepped in, I didn't realize how thoroughly it would change the dynamic between Sandy and me. I was no longer Sandy's go-to person; Sam was. Sandy's and my strongest tie had been severed, as cleanly as my auditory nerve.

SAYING GRACE

I was conditioned to think of grace as a quick blessing before a meal. I remember the words ingrained from my childhood: God is great, God is good, Let us thank Him for our food. *But grace is so much more than a devotional before the fork touches the plate. It is about the act of providing more than food, about providing that which can nourish our souls. Grace is a conversation between you and God.*

Increasingly, I have also come to see grace as being about extending forgiveness. Giving grace to another person is simply forgiving them, unconditionally, no strings attached. Isn't this how God forgives us, even if we don't deserve it? Isn't this how God feeds us—not with an exhaustive accounting, but simply because we are hungry and need to be fed? This is our example, to extend grace to others, and mean it, even when we don't necessarily think that they deserve it. The other person may not do the same, but that does not mean that you do not forgive them, that you do not extend them grace. Staying stuck in unforgiveness only sets you up for heartbreak and bitterness. The person you hurt the most is yourself.

One of my biggest lessons has been about extending grace to myself. To do that, I have to look at myself honestly, name what I have done or not done, and take responsibility. I am still learning the meaning of true forgiveness, and I have to keep doing it over and over again, with family, with friends, with people I have hurt, and with those who have hurt me. Forgiveness is not stagnant. It is always being renewed, and it grows as circumstances change. "Please, dear Lord, Forgive us our trespasses as we forgive those who trespass against us." That may be the message we need to hear, at our tables and in our hearts.

Chapter 17

DEAF AND DEFEATED

In the beginning, I simply didn't grasp how psychologically devastating it was to be unable to hear. One on one I was okay if I was looking directly at the person. But being in any kind of group, even a small group, threw me. I couldn't catch jokes or follow what was being said. I was late to the conversation thread; I was continually stepping on someone else's words. Too often, I was answering the wrong question.

At first, I thought everyone would adjust. I'd just say, "Come over here, I can't hear you." Or I'd tell Sandy that he couldn't yell for me if he was in the other room. But a year passed, then two, and then three, and all those deficits began to add up. Even my friends and family wouldn't remember that I couldn't hear them. For my part, I began to feel like a parrot, repeating the same instructions over and over. I started answering what I thought someone had said. I didn't want to keep asking, "What did you say?"

Gradually, it became easier to nod and smile and not say anything. But when you stop participating in conversations or withdraw from events, after a while, people stop inviting you and asking you to participate. Over time, the tunnel you're in gets darker, the hole gets deeper.

From the injury to my brain, I had lost all the hearing in my right ear and a portion of the hearing in my left, along with my sense of smell. It sounds very cut and dry, but it isn't. It doesn't show up like a limp or a bright red scar. It is all but invisible. If someone sat to my right at the dinner table, I couldn't hear them unless I turned my chair a full ninety degrees and stared directly at their face. If someone walked up on my right side, I would have no idea they were there. Friends, family, Sandy, or my housekeeper would walk up to me in my own home, and I would jump. I still do. It's not that I am afraid; it's that I'm shocked because I have no sound to tell me to anticipate them. If I'm driving a car, I often can't hear what someone sitting to the right in the passenger's seat is saying, and there are numerous times that I've sailed past an exit after they've told me to turn. Nor did I think before about how very much I live in a right-sided world. In my old-school Southern upbringing, the place of honor is on the right side, a man is supposed to walk on the right side of a woman, when you kiss someone hello, it is invariably on the right cheek.

It isn't just the range of sound that I can't hear. It is also consonants, which are, as numerous audiologists have explained to me, the connectors of meanings in a sentence. I have a particularly difficult time with "s"—I often think someone is saying "he" when it is "she." Sandy and I had always watched movies, but after the accident, I largely stopped watching television. Where I had once been able to follow whatever was happening on the screen and flip through a magazine or write letters at the same time, now I had to focus my full attention on the TV.

Wearing headphones was often the only way I could truly follow along. I've come to love Ted Talks, because I can listen to them, then print out and read the transcript and even make a few notes in the margins. The triple processing that I have to do for most ordinary conversation is already built in.

There are so many other gaps associated with my hearing loss. I can't hear a doorbell. I had one friend who arrived at my house, knocked repeatedly, rang the bell, and stood outside the door screaming my name for five minutes. She gave up in defeat, and then had the sudden impulse to send me a text: "Hey, Kreis, just got here." My phone is programmed to flash a bright light when a text comes in. I immediately went to the door; I had been in my bedroom getting dressed, without wearing my hearing aid. For years, I had a service dog named Buddy. Part of his job was to race up to me and bark when the doorbell rang.

Even things as simple as finding my cell phone or setting my alarm are a challenge. If I can't see my phone, I can't find it and calling the number doesn't work. I often sleep through my alarm.

Because I have only single-sided hearing, I also have no idea where a sound is coming from. Many times, it is as if I am chasing a ghost. If my eyes are closed, I don't know where a person is standing. I've tried to block ambient noise coming from another room, only to discover that I've gone to the wrong room and closed the wrong door. If a restaurant is playing background music or has the TV on or is loud, my brain can't distinguish between the background noise and the voice of the person having dinner with me. The same is true at a party or at a large meal.

Our brains are designed to have two-sided hearing—the brain says, "Right ear, you handle conversation, and left ear, you handle the background noise." The ears themselves are divided between the brain's two hemispheres. The right ear is what sends information to the left side of the brain, and vice versa. With single-sided hearing, if there is a lot of noise, the auditory portion of the brain basically shuts down after offering a final set of instructions: "Leave—you can't handle it." It is exhausting to maintain the intense concentration required to separate what one person is saying from all the extraneous sound. When I go somewhere new or find myself in a large gathering, I feel anxious. I start wondering, *What will I be able to hear? What will I miss? How am I going to manage?*

For years, my response was to turn down party invites. I wanted to remain inside the secure zone of my quiet world. I eventually did start going to larger events, but I've learned that I have to take breaks. I duck into the bathroom or head outside for a walk. There are times when I have gone to sit alone in my car so that my brain can rest and I can recharge before I return. I also learned that for important occasions, I need to call ahead to see where I will be sitting.

I have become scrupulous about creating a plan before I arrive. In a meeting, I don't want anyone sitting on my right. When I go to a restaurant, if there are more than two of us, I can't have anyone seated to my right at the table or in the booth, and I always hope the people I'm dining with will speak to the waiter so that I don't have to. I can't understand accents or different speech patterns—it took me years to watch *Downton Abbey*, and I needed subtitles to follow along. Cab and Uber drivers with accents are particularly difficult for me to hear, especially because they are facing away from me.

But the greatest toll, at least in my case, was the impact on how I interacted with my family. Deafness is especially difficult at family events, where everyone gathers and talks over each other. The hardest people to hear were my grandchildren. I cannot hear certain decibels, particularly the higher-pitched sounds of small children and also women. I couldn't understand my grandchildren unless I was looking right at them, and what grandchild wants to stand still and stare in Grandma's face to have an extended conversation? In my "good, better, best" philosophy of life, I felt as if I was a good grandmother, but not a better one, and never the best. I caught snippets of what my grandchildren said, but not everything. So, I tried to just play along. I'm sure there were moments when they wanted my attention and I did not respond. Eventually, I realized that I needed to have each child visit me solo so I could build a relationship one-on-one.

At times, I've fantasized about plugging up my family's ears so they could better understand this new me. I'm certain that I appeared distant, anxious, and frequently not very nice because I was so consumed with trying to navigate my own shrinking world. In addition, I became much more sensitive; while my sight and touch ramped up to compensate for my other losses, so did my emotions. It was the perfect storm: my deafness hurt the people around me, whom I cared about the most, which led to my being hurt in return.

I know now that people outside my immediate family have often thought that I'm at best inattentive and at worst rude, because I look like I can hear. Years after the accident, I was working on a new project with John Perotti, the main foreman for the Alabama construction company that had redone Rose Bay with Sandy and me. John was someone I had known for ten years when we lived in Mobile. One day, I turned to him and said, "John, did you say something to me?" He tightened his jaw and answered, "Yeah," and I explained to him I am deaf in my right ear. A shocked look crossed his face, and he said, "I didn't know that. I thought you had moved to Tennessee and really changed." In so many ways that question I asked Camille immediately after my accident, "Do I look like I can't hear?" is the question that has come to define my life. I look like a hearing person when I am most definitely not.

Well-meaning people often say, "Oh, don't worry, I can't hear that well either," or "My dad can't hear well." But there are many kinds of deafness, and sudden, traumatic hearing loss is not like age-related hearing impairment. You could put a foghorn in my right ear and it wouldn't affect me. Others wonder if I have tried the latest hearing aids. Several years ago, I had a BAHA implant, a bone-anchored hearing aid, for which a titanium bolt is drilled into the skull and a sound device is attached. When I rub my scalp in that spot, I feel something odd, similar to the tip of a Phillips head screw. The theory behind the implant is that by attaching the box to the bone, the vibrations produced by outside noise can be transmitted to the brain—it's supposed to function like surround sound. I talked to a musician who got one, and he said it restored his ability to play music. A teacher said that while she still couldn't hear words and specific sounds, it was the closest thing to hearing. But the implant didn't work for me because the place where my skull fractured and where it was cut open for my surgery never knit back together. It stayed cracked like the Grand Canyon, and the vibration can't travel across the gulf. In addition to the implant, I have a hearing aid with a radio transmitter. It can't translate words, but it can translate sound. But it is uncomfortable and frankly not very effective. Mostly I use the aid designed to amplify whatever sound comes into my "good" ear.

In the course of one home design project, I met a ten-year-old boy who suffered from a hearing deficit. I watched how he moved, his patterns, and the ways that he reacted to the external world. His biggest question for me was if the family playroom for his three brothers and sisters would be near his room, because he needed his own quiet space. I understood what he was saying before he was done asking. After the formal meeting, he invited me to follow him around his house as he showed me his musical instruments and excitedly told me about how much he loved to play the drums, because he could feel the sound when he played. "Watch this," he said as he tapped his sticks against the snares, making his own rhythm in what to everyone else is a surround-sound world.

I am still trying to find my rhythm. Even during the first few years, I never expected that deafness would totally change my life, for although the deafness was sudden, the change it brought about in me was slow. I went from being self-confident, from being able to get things done or find the best people and cheerlead the process, to being a shell of my old self. I couldn't walk into a meeting and bubble over with ideas—I was lucky if I even heard what was being discussed. I always kept an assistant and often used her like a living hearing aid, to follow the conversation, to speak to the waiter in a restaurant, to navigate all the places where I was unsteady and unsure. I no longer walked into a room and enjoyed seeing everyone at a party. I became the woman who snuck out early and talked to as few people as I could manage.

This sticky cocoon of silence envelops me from the second I wake up and ends only when I lay my head down to sleep. Most days, I feel entirely defeated by my deafness. I still make many decisions about what to do or where to go based entirely on whether I will be able to hear.

Not being able to smell is often a source of laughter—I'm not bothered walking past an overflowing dumpster. One of my grandchildren will say, "Oh, that stinks!" And my reply will be, "Not to me." It provides endless amusement that I can't smell or hear farts and burps. But those deficits don't affect relationships. Not being able to hear does.

All of this damage was made worse by the fact that the rest of my life was in flux. I had no routine with friends, my children were scattered, living independent lives of their own. The people I cared about I saw only episodically, never often enough or for a long enough block of time to allow them to adjust to my disability and for me, in turn, to recalibrate my relationships with them. My constant repetition of "What?" and "What did you say?" made me seem at best distracted and at worst head-shakingly stupid and easily dismissed. The extroverted person who loved to design other people's interiors, always hosting family and friends for meals and gatherings, began to retreat into her own walled-off interior life.

Chapter 18

NOMAD

In 1997, twenty years after Sandy and I started Blackberry, I got my first business card. It read *Kreis Beall, Proprietor,* which I defined as everything from COO, chief operating officer, to CBO, chief bottle washer. Sandy was always our chairman of the board. It was no coincidence that I received my business card the year Sam got married and David left for his freshman year at Southern Methodist University in Dallas. My mom "job" was largely complete, and work was what remained.

Five years later, not only could I no longer be Blackberry's hands-on proprietor, but I could not work even part time and expect to be in the flow of the business. On the occasions when I did drop in, I would quickly discover that I had missed a major decision or operational change, and I felt left out. My response was to host my own little pity party, during which I would miss the next issue or operational decision and the entire vicious cycle would repeat.

But while I was no longer an active proprietor, Sandy very much remained the chairman of the board. And that meant we were no longer a team in the way we had been since the start of our marriage. Work had always made Sandy and me "work" as a couple. We were two workaholics, never stopping, always going, two highly functioning business partners, divvying up duties and spheres. Sandy put it best when he said that his priority order (and mine by inclusion) was 1) work, 2) spouse, and 3) our kids. Success was all he and I had known, and twenty-five years of marriage had taught me there was nothing that couldn't be fixed with more hard work. Whenever we came to a fork in the road, a choice between spouse, children, family, friends, or work, Sandy and I chose work every time. Now, without it to cement our partnership, our foundation was slowly being chipped away.

This was something neither of us could articulate. Healthy relationships, I have come to understand, are supported by emotional, intellectual, physical, and spiritual pillars. In our relationship, however, emotional and spiritual communication was missing. We primarily communicated through projects and accomplishments. It was very well-rounded communication in that sphere: we could agree, we could disagree, we could compromise. But it was also results-driven and one-dimensional. We had complete loyalty and trust around a conference table, but without a set meeting topic or an agenda, I couldn't verbalize to either Sandy or myself how I truly felt. We had spent so many years being each other's cheerleader in business, not realizing that loyalty is not the same as intimacy. Now, in midlife, we could not buy intimacy in the same way that we could buy a house, a car, or a rug.

For decades, I had also trained myself to ignore my emotional needs. I assumed they would resolve on their own. I never considered what leaving Blackberry would do to me psychologically, how central Blackberry was to my identity. I never considered how important having a community, like what I had at Rose Bay or had started to build at Blackberry, was. I simply thought, *Oh, I'll just do something else. That will be fun.* I assumed I could become a photographer or start raising bees. But I didn't need a quick replacement. I needed a life reboot, to find the thing that would give me meaning, fellowship, and genuine purpose.

Sandy tried to reach out to me. We started on an endless cycle of projects. From 2002 to 2010, we bought sixteen homes in six states and sold almost as many. Some were total redos; six were completely new builds on empty lots. They were a combination of main houses and vacation houses, and more often than not the furniture, drapery, and lighting had barely been installed before we sold and moved on.

It's easy to write those houses off as an addiction, but that is too simplistic. One of my dear friends from Point Clear says it was just what Sandy and I did; that for us, it appeared completely natural, "like breathing." But in hindsight, I think we were chasing a previous life that had literally gone up in smoke or been drained away in a hospital neurosurgical operating room.

We had an unspoken belief that if we could just do the "right" house, we would simply walk through that new front door and re-create the past. Every problem would be fixed or, like excess furniture, be conveniently put into storage or left behind. Almost to prove that point, after the Pretty Woman house, we purchased a finished, already furnished townhouse in Hilton Head, the place where we had spent so many carefree weekends when we were young and the boys were small, where anything had seemed possible. We visited that townhouse two times before we sold it.

I didn't want to do most of these projects, but I couldn't bring myself to say no. We entertained, I put on beautiful dinners and picnics. Sam's growing household of children visited, and in the moment, it was fun. I'd gear up for a busy two or three days and then everyone would depart and the house would sit empty. A week or two would pass, and I would repeat the same event all over again. It was like running a personal hotel where we hand-selected the guests.

But I did not want to import different people to fill my guest rooms and drink wine and break bread every week or two. I wanted people and real relationships as part of my daily world. More than anything, after the accident, I needed to be in one place. I needed to have a normal life. That was what we had made in Alabama.

Only belatedly did I recognize the real "stuff" that had gone up in flames. In Mobile and Point Clear, our lives were organized around the routine of the school year, the lives of our boys—even our back-and-forth on the weekends had a structure to it because we moved with the same tight-knit group of friends. After our children left home, Camille and Joanne Cooper and I would say that we didn't realize how those years of driving carpools and managing everyone's school needs and activities were some of the best years of our lives. We had so few choices, and yet there was a purpose to everything we did. Now all of a sudden, I was being given every choice in the world, except the choice of good health and the settled rhythm of daily life.

As each year passed, I grew resentful of the building and redoing. I grew resentful of packing up and moving. I grew resentful of how it was all so fleeting. Yet I never said no, never articulated, "This is what I need," never drew a boundary line. Years later, Sam would say to me, "Mom, you were unpredictable. We never knew who we were going to get." And it's true. I wasn't easy to be around. I wish someone had taken me by the shoulders, looked me in the eye, and said, "Kreis, you aren't yourself, and we need to figure out why." But it never happened. I've lived in houses with every kind of rope from kitchen twine to plant ties to motorboat mooring lines and thick, wide braids for porch swings, but I couldn't figure out how to fashion my own lifeline.

Looking back, I was most likely suffering from some post-traumatic stress disorder from the fall, a midlife crisis, and a loss of self-esteem, both socially and professionally. A doctor might have even diagnosed me with depression, but I could not verbalize any of it. How could I not feel right on the inside when externally I had created a beautiful brand that my brilliant son was now running? I had a beautiful family and of course a beautiful home. Yet I believed that I was carrying around what I perceived as a shameful secret about the workings of my own interior life. I felt even greater shame that I couldn't fix it, and that shame worsened each time I put on my armor and faked it. I felt sick and stuck. But how could I complain when to the outside world it looked as if I had everything? It probably looked like I had emotional fulfillment, too, just as it looked like I could still hear.

It was eight years of a patch-and-glue job to keep my most important relationship, my marriage, standing. If Sandy had known how to fix it, he would have. He would have done anything for me. He comforted me as best he could with the limited relationship skills we both had. But he couldn't save me, and I in turn never said anything, because I kept hoping. I hoped that if I made things beautiful and kept living beautifully, I would rediscover what I had lost. But I never did. I could have nice times in all those beautiful houses, but none of them was ever truly home.

Chapter 19

A WEDDING AND A PRAYER

At age twelve, Sam announced that he no longer needed his mother to make his grilled cheese sandwiches. He would do it himself, thank you, and each one would be exactly how he liked it—the bread, the butter, the cheese, each component selected, sized, and cooked just so. He approached the rest of life with that same self-contained certainty. Among his friends on the bay and at school, he was the ringleader, the organizer, the boss of everything. During college, he spent his summers working in different departments at Blackberry. He wanted to learn different facets of the farm. When he decided to study at the California Culinary Academy, I asked him why, and he answered with one sentence: "Mom, California is where everything is happening."

Sam wanted to learn everything. He worked at the Ritz-Carlton Hotel in San Francisco, then at the Cowgirl Creamery, and later did his restaurant internship at the French Laundry in Napa Valley. But he was always thinking ahead and planning. Early in the morning and on his days off, he would ride his bike for thirty, forty, fifty, seventy-five miles through Napa, stopping at boutique vineyards to pass out Blackberry Farm brochures. He started talking to top vintners, telling them about his home in Walland, Tennessee. When he returned to Blackberry and started work in the restaurant, cases of those wines followed—Blount County, Tennessee, had finally become a "moist" county, where alcohol could be served and sold in certain jurisdictions.

Sam had a vision for every part of his life. He knew he wanted a large family, and he knew he wanted to build a house that incorporated the porch and the dining room from Rose Bay as well as the kitchen from the Maple Cottage, and a treehouse fort in the back for his children like the one he had briefly in one of our Knoxville homes. He knew exactly how he wanted to expand Blackberry, adding a second, stand-alone dining space that could also host cooking schools, and planting a kitchen garden nearby, as well as a creamery to make cheese, a wine and spirits cellar, an event space, and a spa.

Most of all, he knew how he wanted to organize his time—"Sam time," we came to call it. He refused to be a slave to emails, so it could take him three weeks to answer. He would stop and spend forty-five minutes on something or someone that mattered to him, knowing the rest could and would wait. He tried not to devote time to things that did not interest him. He tried to never miss an event that involved his children. He was a competitive, near obsessive cycler, so much so that to keep to his cycling schedule and still keep a meeting time, he once showed up to give a presentation to two hundred people in his clip-on shoes and cycling clothes without even pausing to remove his helmet. One night when he hadn't returned from Blackberry, Mary Celeste became frantic that something had happened, until she found Sam in the driveway, asleep with his car in park and the engine still running, a wine book open in his lap. He hadn't wanted to come in until he had read to the end of the section.

In his own way, David was every bit as certain. When he was about twelve or thirteen, he went on a hunting weekend with Sandy, Sam, and some other friends. Everyone was ready and dressed, Sam with his gun perfectly polished and in his full hunting gear. They called for David to come on, and he walked out, barefoot, with a camouflage shirt over his pajamas, and said, "I'm ready." In his mind, he truly was. When David was seventeen, his college counselor told him that the two best schools for his academic needs were University of Mississippi (Ole Miss) in Oxford and Southern Methodist University in Dallas. For David, it wasn't even a dilemma. He told me once, "Mom, you know I'm your city boy." He wanted to live amid gleaming vertical towers and intersecting grids of asphalt, where he would see people at every turn. At SMU, he played varsity tennis as a walk-on. Senior year, he set himself up as a stock day trader, investing his grandparents' gifts and summer job savings, buying and selling from his computer inside his apartment. I joked that I wanted a commission because I had decorated that apartment. After he graduated, Sandy found him a job at a bank in Knoxville. David stayed for four months, then while Sandy and I were on a bike trip, he resigned, rented a U-Haul, and drove to New York. All in all, quite an exit strategy, expertly utilizing the tactics he gleaned from his mom and his dad.

After New York, he tried Atlanta, then Miami, always cutting a wide swath around Blackberry, the place that had absorbed his brother whole. But there was no animus in his choice. Easy, sweet David just knew what he was drawn to. He knew he wanted to marry smart and beautiful Lauren Olsen, a University of Texas alum, three or four years before they walked down the aisle, which they did on August 23, 2008, at Blackberry, eleven years after Sam's wedding and thirty-three years after mine and Sandy's.

Although it was home to us, for Lauren's family from Atlanta, Blackberry meant a destination wedding, and almost all the guests were from out of town. Her mother, Lee, did most of the planning for the wedding day, but I oversaw two events, the rehearsal dinner the night before and a smaller dinner on Thursday for extended family who would be arriving two days early.

I was driving a golf cart one afternoon when I passed Doug Banister taking his usual reflective walk around the edges of Blackberry, alone. I hadn't really spoken to him since that first year after my accident. As my cart drew closer on the path, I suddenly decided that I wanted our Thursday-night dinner for David and Lauren to be a prayer supper. I pulled up alongside him, hit the brake, and said, "Hey, Doug, David and Lauren are getting married, and I was wondering if you could come to our prayer supper to bless the marriage?"

He wasn't my preacher, and I didn't go to his church. He had left the large Fellowship Church with the big screens and had formed his own, much smaller church, All Souls, which met in a multi-use space in downtown Knoxville. Doug might have met David in the ICU, but it had been almost nine years since then and he didn't know Lauren at all. Yet he quickly said, "Certainly."

I don't know if in that moment I had a guardian angel or if I was somehow moved by the Holy Spirit or simply by my own impulsiveness. But in those few minutes, it seemed not only right, but also the only possible thing to do, and I did it. If he'd said no, I'd probably have asked, "Do you know somebody who will?" I told him I would call about the details. We exchanged phone numbers and emails, and just like that, we had reconnected.

Years before, close to Hesse Creek on a small rise, I had decided to build a little white clapboard chapel. Doug suggested we hold a simple service there before dinner. David and Lauren liked the idea. So, in the weeks before the wedding, I was thinking about the Thursday family prayer supper and about seating 185 guests outside my Blackberry house for the Friday-night rehearsal dinner, about how I was going to arrange the tables and do the seating, the menu, the weather, the flowers, and about what I was going to wear.

At that point, in 2008, I still naïvely assumed that marriages just rolled on forever, propelled by their own forward momentum. I assumed happy, loving couples stayed mostly happy and still somehow in love. I thought the smiling photographs from Lauren and David's perfect mountain wedding had captured everything.

Three weeks later, the housing bubble burst, the stock market collapsed, and the bottom fell out of the economy. Three years later, the bubble surrounding my own marriage would burst and then it, too, would be gone.

Chapter 20

RIVER HOUSE

Sandy and I did not give each other gifts. Or more precisely, gifts were not a priority. When anniversaries rolled around, more often than not I would buy something for Sandy and also something for me, have them wrapped, and take both presents to whatever restaurant we had chosen for our celebration. At a certain point, I produced the pretty packages from my bag and we would "exchange" our gifts. Birthdays were the same. I took care of both his and mine. There were times when we would slip onto our seats and Sandy would ask, "So, what are we celebrating?" The night was on his calendar, but the date had lost its meaning. I thought it was a symbol of how well the independent facets of our marriage functioned together, a sign of our partnership roles. Now I wonder if, like all the household tasks that Sandy disliked doing—pulling weeds, mowing the lawn, touching up paint, washing windows, or fixing the squeak in the door—those small, thoughtful gestures are the indispensable maintenance in a relationship, the cumulative way to renew and repair?

Sandy was eminently capable of the generous big gesture. And this is where the accounting gets so hard. On the large things, it was darn near impossible to outdo Sandy Beall. He gave me my vocation in Blackberry. He gave me the gift of taking me home from the hospital and overseeing my care after my accident. Near the time of our twenty-fifth anniversary, which also coincided with my extended recovery, he had a jeweler friend deliver the equivalent of a diamond engagement ring, an incredibly showy cushion-cut diamond that I hadn't asked for but Sandy insisted on. "Try it," he said. When I spent four months in New York at the start of 2009, one Saturday night he surprised me, waiting on the sidewalk in the falling snow as I walked out of *Billy Elliot* on Broadway. I was supposed to return to Blackberry for an event; instead, Sandy came north to be with me. It was probably the most romantic thing he did during our entire marriage. He rarely said *don't do it, don't buy it, don't see it, don't go to it, don't share it.* Which is why it is so hard to think that the final act in our marriage began with something mundane and small.

It is possible to love Blackberry but not want to live there full-time when your grown son is running the place, and that was pretty much where I was at the start of 2009. I was in search of another purpose. I went to New York to take a class, and I loved the outside stimulation and spending four months away. I realized that I was often happier traveling for a weekend, a week, or a month than I was being at my own house. I left thinking it would be better for Sandy and me, and also for Sam, if Sandy and I had a different home.

Among all the places that we had bought and sold since the accident, there was one I had particularly loved. It was in Knoxville, on a bluff overlooking the river, and I had named it the

River House. It was a beautiful old house and we had plans drawn up for its renovation, but we never followed through. Instead we started another project and sold the unrenovated house to a business executive and his wife. Now he was interested in selling back to us. For a second time, we closed on the River House. With the architects, I worked up designs for an updated kitchen, an interior den, a playroom for the grandchildren, a new third floor, and improving the pool. I knew exactly where I was going to install a rose garden. River House was, quite simply, the home of my childhood dreams.

We moved into the garage apartment while the work was being done, and we also went back to Point Clear, where Sandy found us the perfect cottage on the quieter, inward-facing side of the bay. Thinking of Rose Bay, I named it Rose Cottage. I loved this house in a deep, resonant heartbeat type of love. It wasn't antebellum or overly historic; it was the last house at the end of a bumpy lane, a short walk from the church where Sam and Mary Celeste had been married. It was memorable without being showy. We added large windows across the back to absorb the light, the trees, and the water. I had visions of Sam and Mary Celeste escaping to Point Clear with their children. Sandy and I talked about how we would spend our golden years, living four to five months of the year in Point Clear and then the rest of the time back in Knoxville, at River House and also at Elkmont Cottage, a smaller home we were finishing on a lot inside Blackberry.

I was coming up on the ten-year anniversary of my accident, and I finally felt as if I had emerged on the other side of a long, stifling tunnel. I pictured a new life for us where the joy would be built back up. I saw these houses, but River House especially, as our houses of hope.

And then one afternoon in the summer of 2009 during the renovations at Rose Cottage, Sandy and I went for a walk around the neighboring town of Fairhope. I decided to go into a dress shop I hadn't visited for a while. Sandy, who also loves shopping, walked in and sat down on one of the chairs. While I tried on a few things, he began chatting with a young woman who worked there. Sandy is a people person—he will talk to anyone, asking them all kinds of questions. He loves mentoring people, so I didn't think anything about it when he asked what she was studying in college and where she saw herself in five or ten years. Before we left, Sandy offered to give her advice and they exchanged emails.

Sandy looked at her school curriculum online and wrote to her about his ideas for a college major. He suggested that she look into a business program at the University of Tennessee and consider taking a CPA test, which was what Mary Celeste had done, because there is always a good job market for CPAs. I knew he was writing to her. When we were in Point Clear checking on the Rose Cottage renovations, we went back to the dress shop and Sandy talked to her again. Her name rhymed with Alabama, and I began thinking of her as the pretty Alabama girl, "A" for short. He suggested to A. that she consider interning at Ruby Tuesday in Maryville in the summer, but she replied that she didn't know where she would stay.

We had just moved into the River House, and from the time we had lived in Hilton Head all those years ago, we had always opened up our home. So I said, "Well, Sandy, we have plenty of room. She could come live with us." A. wasn't the only young woman we hosted that summer. We had a former WNBA pro-basektball player living with us as well while she was working to start a personal training business. I thought it would be nice for two young women to have each other.

I saw only a single red flag. One morning, A. hopped in the car with Sandy to ride to work. I told Sandy, "You cannot do that. You cannot, as the head of the company, drive an intern to work in your car." In August, A. packed up and left, and to me it was out of sight, out of mind.

Rose Cottage was finished in October 2010, and Sandy and I had a house party in Point Clear to celebrate. The entire weekend something seemed off. Sandy didn't have his usual focus. As I was loading my car to drive back to Knoxville, Sandy said, "I want to stay down here and veg for a few days." I was thrilled. Sandy never took time off. Perhaps this was exactly what he needed, a break. I said, "Yes, do it. That's so good." Of course, we had come in two cars, so leaving and staying behind were easy.

October passed and most of November. We went to Sam and Mary Celeste's for Thanksgiving, and came home sleepy from eating too much turkey and having too much to drink. Sandy lay down on the couch and closed his eyes. I wanted to make a call and my cell battery was dead, so I walked over and picked up his phone. On the screen, I saw a notification. I opened his email, and there was a note from A.: *Dear Sandy, Thanks to you and Kreis for sending me to the Ashram. It was great. It was everything you said.*

I could barely keep reading. For twenty years, the Ashram had been a source of safety and refuge for me, a place of stability and healing. It was where I had gone to begin to get myself back after my accident. It was the place I had gone with Camille when her husband was diagnosed with early-onset Alzheimer's and where we truly talked about hard things. It was a place I had only shared with my closest friends, and where Sandy had finally gone for the first time earlier that year when he turned sixty.

My head was spinning. I was trying to connect the dots, thinking *A. knows about the Ashram, Sandy is staying in touch with her.* Then my mind began scrolling back to our visit to Alabama, and I started wondering if Sandy had seen her then. I shook him awake, and I was furious. "What is this?" I asked, and he answered, "Oh, it's no big deal. You know that we send people to lots of different things." We did, but I had always known what was being done in advance; it had been a joint decision, something we had done together. I asked Sandy if he had seen her after I left Point Clear. He said yes, but that it was "nothing."

I paused. "Sandy," I said, "that is something."

All humans are equipped with an innate fight-or-flight response. I fought first and fled second. I called Bernadette and booked a trip for us to New York and Boston. I did not want to drive anywhere—I wanted that sensation of the plane lifting off from the ground and piercing the higher levels of the atmosphere, of being momentarily lighter than air. I wanted to sleep in a hotel bed with no associations, on crisp, tightly tucked, anonymous sheets, a place where at check-in I was just a reservation number and a credit card imprint. I asked Bernadette because we had been friends for years and because she always knew everything. It turned out that in October, Sandy had been seen walking around Fairhope with A.

I signed Bernadette and me up to do two things: see the play

War Horse in New York, which was at Lincoln Center (with state-of-the-art headsets), and visit the new American wing at the Boston Museum of Fine Arts, where the exterior looked ugly to me but inside were the most perfect gallery rooms I had ever seen.

I thought an itinerary and a schedule would help. It did and it didn't. I veered from being hyperaware of everything around me to walking around in a half stupor. I asked for coffee I didn't finish and ordered meals I pushed away after a few bites. I wanted to imagine everything playing out somewhere else, in someone else's life. But at night, I would shut the door, close the curtains, and feel a heaviness hit me straight in the chest. I didn't hear from Sandy. I didn't call Sam or David, and my sons, preoccupied with their own families and busy lives, wouldn't have known to call me. I began to wonder if I was overreacting.

I also made an appointment to see Nancy Lee, the psychologist in Boerne, Texas. After Bernadette flew home to Knoxville, I waited by myself to catch the first of two flights, because I couldn't fly direct to San Antonio. The early-December weather turned fickle and my connection was cancelled. Stuck in the airport, I called Nancy Lee to tell her I wasn't going to make it, and to see what her schedule was like the next day. But the longer I waited, the more I thought, *I'm just going to go back, I'm going to see if we can work this out.* I called again and cancelled with Nancy Lee, and then I called Sandy, and said, "I want to come home."

DESIGNING A HOME

———◆———

I never went to formal design school. I've always believed that there are other designers who can do it better or who know more than I do. What I have learned is how to live in every inch of a house and to design a house that's meant to be lived in. To me, the most important thing about a vibrant house is living in every room. Use every room every day and those spaces will become like a second skin.

It starts by finding a purpose for each space. If you have a room that sits empty, ask yourself: What would make me use this room? In my current living room, I had two sofas and an assortment of chairs. You could seat the world in there, but I wasn't sitting there. So I took out a sofa and moved my desk in. I enjoy sitting there when I work, looking at living room decorations, rather than the traditional trappings of an office. But using space isn't simply about bringing work into your home. Instead, think about what draws you into a room. For me, it's a fireplace. I love the light, the comfort, the warmth.

When we lived in Mobile on Eaton Square, the boys, Sandy, and I spent our time almost exclusively in the back, in our big den, kitchen, and sunroom. Our charming little living room at the front was neglected until I changed the small fireplace to gas, which would light with the push of a button. Sandy and I started gathering there at night to unwind and talk about our day before we ate dinner with the boys. That room became our personal space where we could take a breath.

I am generally not a good sitter—I like to be doing things—but if I'm going to sit in a house, I want to be by a fireplace or on the porch on a chaise lounge. But each person is different. If you never use your dining room, try installing bookcases or add board games—do something at the table rather than just have a formal meal. There are no rules you have to follow; you just need to think, How can I make this space work for me?

To make your house truly yours, it helps to find the right palette and style for you and for the house. My friend Suzanne Kasler's personal look is more feminine than mine. But on all our collaborative projects, she had focused on my palette, which includes deeper colors like ochre, faded gold, and burnt orange, and mixed old woods. While trends can be fun, remember to honor your personal style. My underlying style is very traditional and that's not likely to change. I want my spaces to work for blue jeans to ball gowns.

A few years ago, a good friend came to me and asked me to give her home an entirely new look, sleek and contemporary. Her old furniture was too "granny." We came up with a design plan, she approved every piece, and then she wanted me to partially install it. When she saw the beginnings of her new contemporary look, she immediately said, "Nope, I want all my old furniture back." She sent the new pieces to her son for his New York City apartment. He loved them. And I was reminded that houses, like the people who live in them, should stay true to themselves. It's your home, and it should be authentically you.

In the hotel business, the rule of thumb is to refresh a space every seven years. I don't think that's practical for a house, but it is a reminder to move things around, refresh something that has gotten tired, replace photographs, recover things that are worn. You may no longer need a play space filled with toys if your kids are bigger, or you may need a different home office setup, or you may have found a new hobby so you need to set aside space or repurpose a console or cabinet. You might want to put in raised *plant beds or grow boxes and start gardening. You might simply need to throw out or donate things you no longer use. Our homes are not static, they are capable of changing and adapting with us.*

Every house I've ever been in, I've started out by asking, How will I live in it? *or* How will my clients live in it? How can the house be lived in now, and how will it work when there is a new baby or when someone grows old? What is right for this space and this place?

Our homes also hold some lessons for us—what is it about ourselves that we would like to update or refresh? Are we sharing all of ourselves, developing all of ourselves? When I prioritized the business of home, what were the spaces that I wasn't living in with my children, my friends, my husband, and also my God? What rooms did I neglect, chasing the god of success? Did I allow the physical inventory to overwhelm my spiritual inventory? Did I even take a spiritual inventory? Because living in a house or a life is about all the ways you can enter and be present. It is about making room for what truly matters to each of us.

Chapter 21

THE POOL AT BETHESDA

David and Lauren had been married for about eighteen months when I got a call from Doug Banister. He was inviting me along with my friend Dee, my longtime Blackberry neighbor who had bought Maple Cottage, to join a women's Bible study group for working women. We both said yes, and we started meeting about twice a month for an hour, talking about the meaning behind scripture stories like the Good Samaritan. But we always began with the question "How's your life going?" After a few times listening to this question, something prompted me to ask Doug if I could talk to him one-on-one. He told me to come to his office downtown by Market Square. It was a small, simple space: a glass door, a single window, his desk in the corner, a wall of books, two club chairs with a table in between. His "beverage station" was a plug-in teakettle. I sat down with my good ear facing out into the room, and I asked him to turn off the little white noise machine because I couldn't hear anything over it.

Unless it was work related, very few people ever asked me

how things were going, or if they did, it was perfunctory, like commenting on the weather. I was just supposed to answer "Fine" or "Great" and move on. So to have someone sit there and ask me about my soul, my being, my thoughts, and my problems was a powerful new experience. I'd also never met a person who could do more with so few words. In ten words or less, Doug makes you want to spill your heart out. And then he listens.

I started by saying "Something's not right." Then I shared my years of accumulated frustrations, particularly about how when I was asked to return to Blackberry to consult and help with specific design projects, I sometimes felt like a third or even a fifth wheel. I talked about internal disagreements over the best way and location to store wine and "whined" about why my ideas weren't immediately embraced. At home for years, with Sandy traveling so much, I had often been a very unilateral decision maker, until that was pretty much my default setting. I sat and talked all about business, and Doug listened and said very little. We met again, and afterward, he sent an email giving me some homework. He assigned John 5:1–14, "The cure of the sick man at the Pool of Bethesda," with the request to come to the next session and tell him what I thought.

The passage tells the story of Jesus going to the Pool of Bethesda, next to the Sheep Pool in Jerusalem. Bethesda, which means "mercy" in Aramaic, was the gathering place for sick people, the blind, the lame, and the paralyzed. One of the men waiting by the side of the pool had "an illness which had lasted thirty-eight years." Jesus asked this man, "Do you want to be well again?" The man replied with a litany of excuses: that he had no one to put him in the pool and that someone else always reached the healing water before he did. Jesus did not say, "Oh, poor you." He did not commiserate. He did not talk about being patient and waiting for a turn in the healing waters. Instead, he simply told the man, "Get up, pick up your mat, and walk around." In the next sentence, John writes, "The man was cured at once." But Jesus did not leave the healing at physical health. Later, the man found Jesus at the temple, and Jesus told him that now he needed to heal his spirit: "See, you are well again. Stop sinning or something worse may happen to you."

I read and reread the passage, and what it said to me each time was "Kreis, it's you who needs healing. It's you who needs to pick up your mat." I could not spend my life waiting for better hearing aids, less crowded rooms, a more responsive child, a more communicative husband, or to wait for meaning to find me, take me by the hand, and lead me in. The passage said to me, "It's you that needs to listen to Jesus. Listen to Jesus if you want to get healed and walk out into your life." The message seemed loud and clear, scary and joyous, all at the same time.

If anyone ever asks me "What is the thing that brought you to faith?" my answer is always the story in the Gospel of John of the sick man at the Pool of Bethesda. That was what I was thinking about in the summer of 2010, into the fall, all the way to that disastrous Thanksgiving night.

When I had called Sandy to tell him that I wanted to come home, he wasn't at River House; he was at Blackberry. That's where we sat down and where he told me there was "nothing" going on. "I'm just mentoring," he said, adding that A. was trying to balance school, work, and family responsibilities, and she didn't have anywhere to turn. He said that he had sent her to the Ashram to be surrounded by a healthy lifestyle.

I told him that the only way mentoring could work was if we both did it, and if when Sandy met with A. I was always there, too. He agreed. Together, we even picked out a two-week tour of Europe for her.

We drove to Point Clear before Christmas and hosted a holiday party. I invited A., and as a Christmas gift I gave her a Bible. Perhaps I was hoping faith would be a comfort to her, as it was increasingly becoming to me. Yet as 2011 began, I could tell that Sandy's mind was not at home. I wondered if he was thinking about A.

Despite my unease that something was wrong, I clung to what Sandy told me when we took our walks together in the winter cold on the stunted off-season grass covering the golf course at Cherokee. He held my hand and said that this could be the best thing to happen to our marriage or the worst.

There are so many ways a relationship can unravel, so many small pulls and loose threads that accumulate over the years when both partners don't share their truths. But I had always thought that Sandy's and my independence was the unshakeable foundation of our marriage—he himself would say that he thought it was great that we treated each other as equals. I believed that the force of our individual strength was part of what made us stronger as a couple. It turned out I was wrong. Need was greater. Or perhaps it can all be summed up in one line that Sandy wrote as part of a self-inventory during his trip to the Ashram when he turned sixty. At the end of his methodical list, he added the question, "Is this all there is to life?" I should have seen that for the gut punch that it was, but I was too caught up in looking ahead, in my own images of how we were going to spend our next chapter.

Week after week, Sandy kept telling me that he loved me, that he wanted to stay together. But I found myself feeling mistrustful, constantly assuming the worst. Eventually, I told him I couldn't live with our current situation, that if we were to stay together and rebuild, he had to write a letter to A. and end it.

He sat down for two days and wrote the letter. In it, he talked about the six most important things in his life. He wrote, "Our friendship has hurt Kreis." He said he hated to end their friendship, given how well she was doing and how much he believed in her, but, he added, "Right is right and wrong is wrong, and there is no in between." It was full of little isms like that, lines like "If you tell someone you're going to do something, do it." Then he sent it.

To this day, I don't know exactly what she said in response, but Sandy told me he couldn't stop communicating with her because she was too devastated. In late May, we went to Texas to meet with Richard and Nancy Lee. We didn't say it, but we both knew it was one more attempt to save our marriage. We talked for four days and Richard wrote his own letter to Sandy, asking how he could put the life he had built on the line for this relationship. On day five, Sandy said, "I can't give up seeing her."

But I believed that if I just waited long enough with my mat by the healing water, someone or something would come along and carry Sandy and me in. I thought, *I'm going to trust Sandy and we are going to work this out.* Or as I told Nancy Lee, I believed he was going to come to his senses.

We played that game for a month, walking around like two imposters, following the preset outlines of our lives. We went to Point Clear because we were hosting a Fourth of July party. After all those years with our kids, our little group was returning with squealing packs of grandchildren in their swimsuits, carrying their crab traps or sand pails. My fridge was stuffed with food and alcohol in preparation for the party, after which we would watch fireworks light up the sky. It was the night of July 2, and Sandy and I were watching a movie after dinner. Something about the movie made me turn to Sandy and ask him the one question I had not asked in all our months of counseling and agonizing: "You don't want to be married, do you?" He answered with one word: "No."

I didn't say anything in reply. I walked out of the room, took half an Ambien, and crawled into the guest room bed. It was one-thirty or two a.m. when I woke. I got in the car and started driving the 532 miles home. As soon as the sun was in the sky, I called Doug, told him what had happened, and asked if he could meet me at my house. He said yes, but only if someone else was there. So I called Bernadette and asked her to come.

As much as Sandy and I had been imposters in our marriage, for the last month, I had also been an imposter on my own. Week after week, I had sat and read the Bible with Doug and said nothing. That morning, Doug talked to me about what I had gone through, not the painful individual details, but the larger framework. He didn't bash Sandy. He talked to me about how the sin of lying and deceit rips a human being apart worse than almost anything. I remember him saying how death is easier on a partner's psyche than being lied to on purpose. He articulated my hurt.

Doug left, but Bernadette stayed. She moved into my house and stayed with me for a week. I couldn't eat, I couldn't sleep. I started pacing in circles inside my closet like a zoo animal in a cage. Sandy called Richard and Nancy Lee, and their advice was that we take a thirty-day break, thirty days of no contact. "Don't do anything," Nancy Lee told me. "Just breathe."

I hired a moving company and moved all of Sandy's clothes out of the River House. I sent all of his things to a small house in the Sequoyah Hills section that David and Lauren had lived in while David completed a management course. The house, still fully furnished, was sitting on the market. Now it was going to be Sandy's. At least for the next thirty days.

I had to tell my children. I didn't know if Sandy had called them, but I needed to tell them in person. Sam and I ran into each other on the driveway in front of the Oak Cottage, the check-in and concierge building at Blackberry. We stood on the asphalt as guests pulled up and Blackberry bellhops unloaded their luggage and ushered them inside. I said, "Sam, I've got to tell you what's going on." Then I gave him the short outline of what had happened and ended it by saying, "Dad and I are separated." Sam nodded in his solemn, thoughtful, wise-beyond-his-years way. Then I called David and Lauren, and they immediately told me to come and visit them in Miami.

I arrived in the humid, enervating South Florida summer heat more like a walking zombie than a mother. My mind felt stalled, incapable of thinking about much else aside from putting one foot in front of the other, but that didn't matter to David. My sweet and easygoing son did everything he could to take care of me. Being welcomed into David's world and seeing the life my son had created for himself—the family he was building, the friendships he cared so deeply about, and the community he was a part of—was like a light in a dark room. We never talked about Sandy or my crumbling marriage, we didn't have to. Neither one of us would have known what to say. Instead, David and Lauren would take me out to eat, we would walk around, we would look at art. It was exactly what I needed.

But then at the end of the day, when I was alone again, I would get in bed and think, *What am I going to do?*

I had no idea and no plan. All I could do was pray.

The first time I saw Sandy, it was a mistake. His mother had been hospitalized for a surgery, and I coordinated my visit to see her with Sandy's sisters, to make sure Sandy wasn't around. But when I went a second time, as I pushed in on the right side of the double hospital door to enter, Sandy pushed out on the left to exit. It was like a scene from a movie. We passed face-to-face, and we laughed. He called and we talked, one of those easy conversations that can flow between two people with thirty-six years of history. I invited him to dinner at the River House, with our grandkids. We grilled by the pool, and it was how I imagined our life together would have been. I saw a glimmer of hope that this separation was a good thing. Our thirty days were not up, but going forward, I believed we were still Kreis and Sandy, that this episode was in fact going to be the best thing to happen to our marriage, and that together we were going to grow into something better. It was, I told myself, all going to be okay.

Chapter 22

BAPTISM

That August, Doug had told me that he wanted me to be baptized. I was a little stunned, but I asked when, and he said that he did adult baptisms twice a year, so either in September or at Easter. I immediately said Easter, because I wanted to put it off. Doug's next words were "I take that back. I think you need to be baptized in September," adding that he's found when someone has a spiritual awakening, it's best to seize the moment. I said okay, and then Doug told me I would have to give a speech. "You have to say what your life was like before you became a believer, why you became a believer, and what is the difference."

Sandy gave speeches, Sam gave speeches. I did not give speeches. But I went up to my office over the garage in River House. I had a botanical photo studio with northern light, a digital darkroom, and office space that overlooked the river. I sat, looking out at the water, and I wrote. My first sentence said that I had been through "three life-changing events in the last fifteen years." I talked about Rose Bay burning to the ground. I talked about losing my hearing and my confidence, my insecurities about answering slowly and speaking slowly and having the rest of the world assume that my brain was slow as a result. I wrote about God coming to me eighteen months earlier, and about how, following my accident, Doug had prayed for ten years that I would fall in love with Jesus. I wrote about talking to Doug, and how he emailed me the scripture story of Jesus at the Pool of Bethesda. "I asked Jesus to heal me," I wrote. Then I thought about that healing, and I decided, "God has forgiven me for not managing personal conflict and for harming my family relationships. God's forgiveness is the greatest gift I will ever receive."

I wanted to tell everyone there that my faith was "direct and simple." I called myself "a Christian in progress." And only then did I get to my third life-changing event, the one that had happened on July 2. I still have the words, exactly as I typed them into my computer, courtesy of that typing class I took all those years ago when Sandy picked me up for our first date. "My husband told me he didn't want to be married to me, and I moved him out of our home. He wants to decide what he wants to do for the rest of his life. We are separated, but we call it a sabbatical. Sandy and I have been married thirty-six years." And I wrote, "Sadly, it was only after Sandy left that I was able to fully grasp how much he means to me. Our separation is by far the worst thing that has ever happened to me. My whole world totally fell apart, and tonight words are still inadequate to accurately share this personal devastation."

I had never been this honest with anyone before, not even with myself. Now I was going to tell a group of people, some family, some friends, some relative strangers, that "I pray for my marriage each day," adding, "God comforts me. God time is different than human time. Troubles just don't go away immediately. If that were so, I would only turn to God out of a desire to be relieved of pain and not out of my love for Him. The comfort that God gives me is strength, encouragement, and hope to deal with life. God has blessed me with perseverance."

I ended my talk with what I recognize now was the beginnings of my own personal prayer: "As I grow in faith, I have learned to rely on God daily and to trust His time frame. Trust, patience, peace, forgiveness, hope, kindness, and love are everything as I follow Jesus. The Bible says, 'God may bring us sorrow, but His love for us is sure and strong. He takes no pleasure in causing us grief and pain.' And like Jeremiah said, 'The Lord is all I have, I put my hope in Him.' I agree with Jeremiah—you don't know that God is all you need until God is all you got. But that is all I need, because God is taking care of me."

"In the past fifteen years I lost my house, my health, and my husband. And I felt like I had lost everything until I became a believer. I stopped focusing on what I had lost and started focusing on what was always there. God and His love. God will never leave me."

Sometimes it's simple when another person tells you what to do. In a few well-directed words, Doug had asked me to tell the truth about my life, and I had said yes. When I read the final version to him, sitting in his office, he didn't say anything. "Did I not do it right?" I asked. "Well," he finally said, grinning, "most people just write up a short paragraph." But I wasn't living a short paragraph. I was tired of putting up the facade of a perfect life.

I invited forty people, friends and family, to come to my full-immersion baptism, held in a city park, the dunking to take place in a public pool. All those years before, when I had told Sandy that I wanted a swimming pool rather than an engagement ring, I never would have predicted that this would be the pool to which I would be led. I asked my boys and my daughters-in-law, my grandchildren, my parents, and Sandy's parents to be there. I don't know what they expected, but my talk was not what they thought they were going to hear. My grandchildren sat and cried because they didn't know about Sandy's and my separation. All they knew was that the previous month, everyone had come to a cookout of tenderloin and vegetables at River House, and Yaya and Papa were there together.

After my public baptism, which included that public confession of my own fragility and the fragility of my marriage, I followed one of the most deeply ingrained patterns of my entire life: I exited. With Camille, Mary Celeste, and my eldest grand-daughter, Cameron, I headed for Peru to climb Machu Picchu, the famous ancient Inca ruin.

The idea for the trip had been born before that dreadful July 2 day. I was talking with friends who live for part of their year in a Wyoming cabin with no electricity and ride mules in the mountains. They were telling me about their latest adventure, hiking to Machu Picchu. I immediately replied, "I want to do that."

I had started planning the trip in June to depart in October. We were going with a group and we would hike for five days along the old Inca trail to the ruins eight thousand feet above sea level. Mary Celeste and I had never traveled together, and I wanted to do something with my granddaughter, Cameron, who was now thirteen, and with Camille.

Every night for more than seven years Camille had been caring for her husband, Happy, who was reaching the end of his struggle with early-onset Alzheimer's. The last event he had attended was David and Lauren's wedding, where he had been unable to speak and his gait was unsteady. He rode in a golf cart, lifting his face to the sun and the breeze. Camille did everything for him. Her children told her it was time for her to take a trip. It seemed as if it would be good for all of us.

Sandy and I continued to talk to each other and see each other every few days, and the talking didn't change when I reached Peru. Our itinerary was to hike the ancient Inca trail to a different guesthouse each night. All of them were electrified thanks to the constant whir of a gas-powered generator—I can only imagine the treks to get the gas to each guesthouse. Most nights, I called Sandy to check in. During one conversation, he told me it was time for him to leave Ruby Tuesday. He said, "Kreis, I just can't stand it. I don't agree with what's going on and I have no control. There's nothing I can do. I think I'm just going to retire, because I'm over it." I sat holding the phone, tears running down my cheeks.

After I hung up, I sobbed. They were not tears for what Sandy had said, the end of an era with the business he had built from nothing when he was still in college. They were grief-stricken sobs for what he didn't say. Since Thanksgiving, nearly eleven months before, Sandy had continued to talk about "us," about our future together. But that night, he only talked about "his" future. He said nothing about the two of us, about Sandy and Kreis walking off together into the sunset. It was all about cutting a cord and his next steps. I could feel it, because when it came to business, Sandy and I still spoke the same language. It was the one topic where I always intuitively felt the truth.

The next morning, there was nothing to do except get up, dry my tears, put on my best face, and continue our uphill climb.

Before we left, Camille had asked what I was packing. "Are you bringing any rain gear?" I told her we were out of the rainy season and I wanted to travel light. Translation: no rain gear. My call had been the right one. We had made it to the last stage of the trail, the hike to the ruins, and all the way, the skies had been a beautiful blue. Our group set out early, and the morning portion of the trail was a relatively easy, slow ascent. We stopped for lunch and suddenly the bright blue sky was overwhelmed by dark gray clouds. We returned to the trail and when we were too far along to run back to any shelter, the heavens opened up. The rain fell in fierce, hard sheets. Everyone else pulled rain gear from their packs, except for me. Our guide started talking to himself under his breath. I don't know any Spanish or local Peruvian dialects, but I'm pretty sure he was saying some version of the universal concept of "idiot." That was certainly what I was thinking about myself. He quickly produced a roll of trash bags from his pack and began to wrap them around me, until I looked like the designated referee for a middle school cafeteria food fight.

Below me on the trail, Camille was dry in her rain gear, but her hiking boots had become waterlogged and her feet were being rubbed raw. She had fallen behind our little charge-ahead group. Damp and dripping, I sat down to wait. Before, I was always a race-the-mountain hiker. At the Ashram, I had not given a second thought about leaving Camille in the middle of the pack. We would meet up later, and I would make my better time. But suddenly being in the lead was not the point. Had I fallen behind, Camille would have waited for me, and done it as if she had planned to. It took a rainstorm on a mountain in Peru for me to understand Jesus' words

---

"The first will be last and the last first."
To receive love, I had to stop counting.

I had to stop eyeing the finish line. First or last, Camille and I would walk this path together.

When we caught sight of each other, I could hear her laugh, followed by "There you are, my trashy friend."

The trail ended at a spot appropriately named the Sun Gate. From it, we looked down to the ancient complex of Machu Picchu, a self-contained city of dwellings, temples, and terraced farms, abandoned six centuries ago. The Incas who'd laid the stones and built this place no doubt never expected their way of life to crumble. No one starting out does, not Camille, not Mary Celeste, not Cameron, and most certainly not me. No one sends you out into the world and says, "Expect ruins." But here was an entire mountaintop telling me otherwise.

We had made it to the summit. It was now time to come down and go home.

Chapter 23

LIGHTS OUT

I sometimes wonder if Doug wanted me baptized in September because he knew what was coming far better than I did.

After I returned from Peru, Sandy and I limped along for two weeks in a peculiar limbo until one Saturday night when we went to dinner with his parents and my parents. Following the Sandy Beall dictum of *Get in the door first,* we ate early and finished early, and when we headed to our separate cars, I decided to follow him home. It was a short drive: turn out of the restaurant onto Northshore Drive then two more turns and suddenly I was pulling in behind Sandy in his driveway. I had no plan. I hopped out, and Sandy said, "What are you doing here?" I answered his question with my own. I said, "So, are we going to stay married or get a divorce?"

Sandy's reply was "I'm writing you an email."

Of all the sentences that could have sent me over the edge, that was it. I raised my voice and I said, "Sandy Beall, we've been married for thirty-six years. You can tell me right now in person. Do you want to be married or not?"

He answered me again with one word, "No." It was the same answer he had given me in July, but this time I heard it.

Months and years of pent-up frustration, anger, hurt, and lies combined in that one moment of truth. On instinct, I pulled back my right arm, and like a spring, released my fist, connecting directly with his nose. As fate would have it, I was wearing the large diamond ring he bought me following my accident, the get-better, twenty-fifth-anniversary, and engagement ring rolled into one. The stone's hard, finely cut point connected with the bridge of his nose like a stiletto. Sandy turned and walked away, blood running between his fingers. I followed, flailing at him, pushing him toward the grass, crying out, "Sandy, what are you doing?"

But truly, what was *I* doing? I have read stories of grieving spouses, parents, even children who start pummeling the complete strangers tasked with notifying them of a loved one's death, the message being so awful that they must sin against the messenger. In that one word, *no,* Sandy was delivering the news of the final passing of our marriage. We were broken, but I didn't want thirty-six years to end prettily or easily. I wanted to fight for my family, so I literally fought back. It was the most out-of-body experience of my entire life.

Sandy didn't say a word; he just kept walking into the house, holding his nose. I followed. I lifted the front hall mirror off the wall and threw it on the floor, where it shattered. Then I walked to his desk and with my arm swept everything, files, papers, pens, photographs, onto the floor. It was blind, furious emotional instinct. Ruins for something ruined. After that, I turned around, marched to my car, and drove home.

I called Dee, my friend and Bible study partner, from my kitchen. I was hoping she was home, but she was in Hilton

Head. She told me to call Sam. The country star Emmylou Harris was playing a concert that night at Blackberry, and I was told, "Sam can't come to the phone." I hung up. I could feel my whole body shaking. I called back and said, "Find Sam and have him call his mother, please." Thank goodness for "Sam time." The same boy who would wait weeks to return an email because he had what he perceived as more pressing things needing his attention was also the person who in the midst of hosting a concert, would stop everything and call his mom. He told me to come to Blackberry. I threw some things in a bag and started driving.

For much of our marriage, Sandy and I had matching cars, a sort of automotive uniform. When we opened Blackberry, we had matching Volkswagen Rabbits. Later it was Land Rovers, although I had so much trouble getting mine serviced in Alabama that I traded it in for a practical and much more common minivan. At this particular moment, we each had Mercedes SUVs—boxy, responsive, four-wheel-drive cars—and Sandy had bought both of them. Mine was white with a tan interior, while he had a black one. During our separation, we had kept our matching cars, as if somehow it signified that we were still one unit.

I drove to Blackberry, parked, and walked into the Barn. The concert wasn't being held on a traditional stage; instead everyone was sitting at dining tables or booths. Mary Celeste and the kids were tucked away at a back booth. I slid in, absentmindedly picked up my granddaughter Rose, and put her on my lap. I smiled and nodded and listened to the music as if everything was just right in the world.

What I didn't know was that Sandy had also driven to Blackberry, but I had gotten there first. In the darkness, he saw the bright white of my car and turned around. There we were, two wounded, childish parents seeking comfort in the home of our grown son.

I stayed at Blackberry that night, got up the next morning, and drove to Knoxville. Young Sam had a flag football game at Lakeshore Park. I went to watch, and Sandy was there, too, sitting by himself, his back propped against the chain-link fence, looking down at his iPad, just as he did during most of the kids' games. I walked over and asked, "Did I break it?"

There was a Band-Aid across the bridge of his nose. "No," he said, "It's just a cut." Then he looked up and added, "You beat me last night. You beat me to Blackberry." It was the last thing with Sandy that I "won."

Whenever times got tough, Sandy always worried about Ruby Tuesday failing. He never put it in terms of personal ego, but he talked about all the people who depended on him, the thousands of employees, shareholders, the diners, the distributors. He could think in huge numbers relating to salaries and payments. He felt a keen duty to all of them. It was the small numbers he didn't always see, the two of us in our marriage, and the four of our sons and their wives, the four, soon to be five, and later seven of our grandchildren. He didn't dwell on what would happen to our family if our marriage failed or what the costs would be.

I went to see my attorney the next day. Within six months, the divorce was finalized. Thirty-six years, done.

Chapter 24

A GREAT PRUNING

Dee's husband, who is a CEO himself, told me, "Kreis, you got fired by Sandy, and once Sandy Beall fires someone, he never looks back."

It was true. I had lost my job of a lifetime, and all that remained was to work out the severance package. Much later, Sandy told me that it was simply time for him to move on. In one of our most honest conversations, he explained that "subconsciously" he wanted more freedom, more time to focus on "self" and to be "more in control" of his life. "Our marriage," he added, "was an obstacle" to that process. To Sandy, "our story isn't about me leaving you for any one person at all, it was about wanting a new phase of my life, a new start and the hope of more happiness." To me, some of the most telling words are the ones he wrote in an email seven years after our legal papers were finalized. Sandy reminded me, "I told you once what some very bright money managers said, that ninety percent of all successful entrepreneurs end up in divorce in their late 50s and 60s as they face the end of business, having neglected their marriage, grown apart, had everything, and yet had little. It happened to me also."

The legal papers were ready in April, there was no drawn-out haggling, Sandy was exceedingly generous in how our assets were divided. For once, he and I rode together in the car to sign the final documents. I had told him, "We got married together. We are going to get divorced together, too." But as the appointed Thursday morning drew closer, I didn't want to go alone. I asked Doug Banister to come with us. We think so much about witnesses to a wedding. There is even a space for their names on a marriage license. Often, the clergy officiating will ask the entire congregation to bear witness to the union of the bride and groom. But divorce usually happens mostly alone in a closed-door room, with a judge, a clerk, and a black or blue ink pen.

That day was a spring thunderstorm morning, thunder, lightning, and sheets of driving rain. It was dark and raining so hard we could barely see out the windshield. Sandy wanted to leave at seven a.m. so we would be the first people at the courthouse, but even he had to go slowly, and what should have been a thirty-five-minute drive seemed like an eternity. I liked that it was raining. It was as if the sky was grieving along with me. I sat completely still. Sandy was fidgety. Doug asked if he could pray for us. Five minutes with the judge, we signed a paper, and our entire married life was wiped away. After, I sat in the car and dabbed at my eyes. We rode back in silence.

The same storm, in all its fury, had passed across the hillside at Blackberry that morning—Sandy has long said that one of his favorite things to do at Blackberry is sit on the gooseneck daybed in the living room, look out over the mountains, and watch the lightning and rain as a storm rolls in.

Standing outside the guesthouse, the first new building Sandy and I had built together at Blackberry, was a maple tree. It had been there since we bought the property, but that morning, lightning hit it. Its largest limb was severed and had smashed into a guest room, shattering the windows. The center of the tree had caught on fire from the ferocity of the strike, its shaft had split, and wisps of smoke rose from where the electric jolt had incinerated the wood. I saw it as soon as I reached Blackberry. The tree would never add another ring of life to its trunk, and in that moment, I felt as if it were speaking directly to me.

For decades, Sandy and I had lived life looking forward. It was never *What are we doing now?* but *What are we doing next?* and *Where are we headed in three years, five years?* Sandy loved spreadsheets and projections. We were not people who said, "Hey, it's cold outside—you want a cup of hot chocolate?" Or "Let's go watch the sun rise." "Let's plant some flowers." "Let's go see Mom." "Let's take the grandkids on a picnic." Instead, we had a happy little business life and we filled every second with that.

Now I could not imagine the future. I could hardly function in the present. I had entered into a season of overwhelming and mind-numbing sadness. All I could do was simply remember to keep breathing. I spent hours sitting on the floor of my closet, frozen, unable to move, much less dress myself. I kept asking myself, *How are you ever going to trust anything or anyone ever again?* I didn't know how to be divorced. I couldn't wrap my mind around the fact that Sandy wasn't there anymore, and he wouldn't be tomorrow, or the next day, or the next year. Every time I saw him, it was as if the scab had been ripped off all over again.

Divorce was not something that happened just to me, but to

my whole family. Season after season of rituals abruptly passed into oblivion. It was the end of everyone being together for Thanksgiving and Christmas. We would have to do a dance of separate lunches and dinners, time together marked off in calendar slots. It was the end of my presence at Sandy's parents' family dinners and Beall family reunions, at Sam and Mary Anne's anniversary parties, and the overflowing family Christmases in Sam and Mary Celeste's home. I abdicated holiday dinners, driving to Camille's in Alabama or to my daughter-in-law Lauren's family in Atlanta. Not because I was no longer welcome in Knoxville, but because I found it too painful to go. Before each event, I thought I would be strong enough, that it wouldn't be so hurtful. Then about three days before, I would realize, like a deep stab, that I couldn't do it. I would text whoever was in charge or just call Sandy's mom and say, "I'm not going to be able to come." I never made up excuses, and Mary Anne always said, "I understand." But *I* didn't fully understand, and deep down I felt jealous that they were still together while I was on my own.

Even our family's annual Christmas hike up to the top of Mount Le Conte in the Smoky Mountains only existed in the past tense. I did not need to put together a pack full of provisions or lay out warm gloves and extra-thick socks. I simply absented myself. Small rituals, such as watching our grandkids' games, also changed. Like opposing teams facing off, Sandy and I would no longer share a single bleacher or place our folding camp chairs side by side. Instead, we settled into opposite encampments. I felt like the losing player in a hard-fought tennis match, forced to stay for the trophy presentation but desperate to exit the court.

That fall, Sandy officially retired from Ruby Tuesday. In an interview, he said, "I don't have regrets because I don't look back. I don't dwell on the past. I try to learn from it. I've made a lot mistakes but those aren't regrets because I learned from them." I, however, had enough regrets for both of us.

In the midst of this despair, I continued to read scripture and to pray. Doug had steered me toward another passage in John, Chapter 15. It reads, "I am the true vine, and my Father is the vinedresser. Every branch in me that bears no fruit, He cuts away, and every branch that does bear fruit, He prunes to make it bear even more." After all those years spent in my rose gardens, pruning and watering, feeding and cutting back, I immediately recognized those words. Pruning is crucial to the health of the vine, but I had never thought about metaphorical pruning as something that might take place in a person. I had never thought that cutting away and paring back might lead to each of us bearing new fruit.

I felt as ugly as those single sticks of bare-root roses that I had planted at Rose Bay all those years ago, yet I remembered that after care and a wintering-over, one by one, they had started to put out stems and then fragile green leaves and eventually blooms. I knew that blind shoots, bits of growth that have no buds, have to be cut off so that the rose can direct its energy to producing billowy flowers rather than a mass of leaves. If I waited, if I could pass through my own pruning, perhaps I, too, might produce some kind of flower or fruit.

"Dear Doug," I wrote in response to this particular assignment. "I relate to John's words describing God as the Master Gardener. I know what a rose looks like in the winter when it is bare of all foliage, and the Master Gardener looks at the branches and knowingly removes dead branches and leaves the branches that have potential. Then spring and summer come, and the rose bears its fruit. When I think of what God is doing in my life, I remember the hard winter in Tennessee of 1993. Two magnolia trees at Blackberry froze. They were twenty feet tall at the time. We simply cut them to the ground hoping that there was some life left in the roots. You know what? Today they are over sixty feet tall. We pruned them just out of hope. And so it is with my life, Doug. I'm beginning to produce fruit thanks to God's thoughtful pruning."

HOLIDAYS—WITH OR
WITHOUT FAMILY

When you work in the service business, as my family does, Christmas often doesn't come on December 25. Add to that generational and geographical differences, and celebrating often has to happen on an entirely different week—December 11 and December 17 have been favorite dates of ours for smaller family Christmases without the full trimmings or tables of food and lush decorations, but with plenty of love.

Although I love my tree and my ornaments and hanging wreaths and stringing garlands, when I look back, some of my most memorable holidays had very few of those things. They were often the smallest events, with the least amount of paper and presents. My favorite in many ways happened almost a half century ago, when Sandy, Sam, David, and I took a trip to Beaver Creek to ski. It snowed so hard that we couldn't even get out to the slopes on Christmas Day. Instead, we sat around in our pajamas and played an epic game of Monopoly, which David won. It was a spontaneous, totally authentic day. I remember another early-December Christmas with Sandy, our two sons, three grandchildren, and our parents in Maryville. There was nothing fancy—it was December 11, so not even every house or apartment in the neighborhood had a tree, but we paused and had our Christmas together.

The same was true with the easy, pared-down Thanksgivings we spent at the hunting camp in Alabama with Camille and her family, kids and dogs running in the grass, eating our turkey on picnic tables, everyone outside for the entire day, family blended with friends. To this day, I always try to go back to Alabama at *some point during the holiday season to be with my friends who became like family.*

And then there are the holidays you are privileged to attend. My dear friend Brenda's companion, Charlie, was in the hospital in New York City for five months for cancer treatment, and the treatment coincided with Christmas. Nothing gave me more joy than to fly to New York, my suitcases stuffed with pillows, throws, and ornaments from her home in Tennessee. In their temporary apartment, we hung stockings, decorated a tree, and cooked Christmas Eve dinner, Charlie's first meal out of the hospital. For weeks afterward, they kept their glowing, decorated tree—its lights like a perpetual light of hope.

Wherever you are and whoever you are with, on whatever day it happens to be, holidays are brightest when they are about joy and love.

Chapter 25

THE SHED

For the first time in my life, I didn't know where I would live. My divorce agreement stipulated that I could live in River House for three years, all expenses paid. Sandy wanted me to stay because he knew how much I loved that house. But it was like living under the ticking of a giant clock. I didn't want to sell, yet at the same time, I was afraid of what would happen in three years if I couldn't sell the house. Sandy and I still owned it fifty-fifty. How could I buy him out and absorb that much debt? How was I going to pay all the taxes and all the maintenance costs? And did I really love the house, or did I love the now vanished idea of Sandy's and my home, the idea of us together with our grandkids?

So when an executive moving to Knoxville said he was interested in my house, I gave him the alarm code and told him to go and look around. That night, I talked about it with Sam and Mary Celeste when we were having dinner with the kids. Sam thought for a moment and said, "There might be a building lot available at Blackberry." All the private home lots had been sold, but a woman whose husband had gotten sick was looking to resell. I bought the lot and started designing a house with the architect Keith Summerour. Then the sale of River House fell through. So now I had a too big house in town and a second house under construction, which I had named Le Conte, after the six-thousand-foot mountain in Tennessee.

I decided I had to sell River House. I signed the listing papers with an old friend from the days when Sandy and I went on our first dates. He had photos done and a video made. We put it on the market for one week, but I couldn't stand the thought of people walking through my house, talking about it, asking me about it. It was like advertising Sandy's and my failure. Psychologically, it was too much. I took it off the market, which solved absolutely nothing.

Ironically, what sold River House was my deafness. As part of my effort to craft a new life, I joined the board of the Knoxville Museum of Art. Our most recent executive committee meeting had been in a restaurant, where I struggled to hear anything over the background noise. For our next meeting, I suggested that everyone come to dinner at my house and sit on the veranda, where I had a fighting chance of keeping up with the conversation. The following morning, one of my fellow committee members called and asked, "Would you be interested in selling your house?" I vacillated. I finally said, "Sure, I'll give you the code to come look," but she said she'd like me to show her around. She also asked if she could bring her interior designers. The next day I was at Blackberry, and she called to ask if she could show her husband. The following day was Friday, and she called again to ask if she could show her children. On Sunday, she said they wanted to make an offer. I gave her a fair number, which was still selling it at a loss after all the renovations, but Sandy and I could divide the proceeds, and I could start over. She agreed, and we shook hands. After some forty houses, this was the first time that I had finally sold a home on my own.

Along with my first sale, I also had my first official paid job. Sam asked me to return to Blackberry as director of design. My project was to work on the design of a nine-thousand-square-foot spa, which was an enormous undertaking for Blackberry, as well as oversee the interior design for private houses being built on Blackberry property and go off-site to provide design services for our guests' personal homes. It was the first time Blackberry design was available for hire by an outside client. In addition, the design team was in charge of all Blackberry Farm interiors. The family design relationship had come full circle. When I started out, I had complete faith in my mother to make things beautiful. There was never a doubt or a question. Now Sam was showing that same faith in me.

I look back and I see how much my son had grown. Unlike when Sandy and I ran Blackberry, Sam clearly laid out my role. I knew where my office was and what my responsibilities were. Because of my history at Blackberry, no one questioned my qualifications. I could contribute. At the same time, there was so much in it for me. I needed to be busy. I needed to be surrounded by energetic young people in a positive, giving environment, and that was exactly what the design team offered. Most of all, I needed to be needed.

I was also tired of moving. Sandy had already chosen the pieces that he wanted from our life together, and now I was left with furniture from Alabama and from Knoxville converging on my new house at Blackberry. I furnished the upstairs with an assortment of things from the River House, while much of my Alabama life was piled in the basement. The house was great for parties and guests, but I always knew it was going to be temporary. I had no history in this house. It looked good, but it was just a house. The best part had been the design and building process.

I knew the house I did want, the small, original turn-of-the-century farmhouse—Blackberry's original homesite—where Sam and Mary Celeste lived when they were first married and where I had lived during my "sabbatical" year when the boys were at boarding school. It was nestled in the valley, away from Blackberry's main buildings. Down a winding road, around a bend, and suddenly there it was, with a vast meadow sweeping behind it and off to the right a cluster of working spaces, a barn, a chicken coop, and a small shed. Beyond it flowed the creek passing underneath a covered bridge, while the edges of the Smoky Mountains rose in the distance. It looked like a storybook farm, although by then I certainly did not have a storybook life. The house itself was currently being used as Blackberry's spa, but the spa was moving. After a full renovation, the white paint farmhouse would be perfect. When someone looking for a home at Blackberry made an offer for Le Conte, I sold it furnished. It took me all of two weeks to pack and leave. But I would be homeless until the farmhouse was complete.

There was one space available at the time. It was that shed, a windowless wooden outbuilding, eighteen by twenty feet, sitting on a slight bow in the land just across the road from the farmhouse. It had that rough-hewn look of so many practical farm buildings. It was built for a purpose, to do a job. There was no ornament or artifice, just vertical board fit side by side, the cast-off pieces from some larger project, salvaged and repurposed, and a bit rougher for the wear. The top was red metal so in the winter the snow and ice could slide right off. I had passed the building for decades, but one morning not long after my divorce, as I walked the grounds, I stopped. I circled the exterior and thought, *I could turn this into a bedroom.* This was before Le Conte, and usually when I came to Blackberry and didn't want to drive back to Knoxville, I would try to stay in an unbooked guest room. But that was hit or miss. With the shed, I would have my own space.

I called Jon Hawker with Hickory Construction and told him I wanted to create a small loft and a tiny bathroom, with a narrow space for a mini fridge and a coffeemaker. The sleeping area was barely large enough to hold a bed, a lamp, a chair, a chest, and a few books. I added a real door and windows, but from the roadway it still looked like an outbuilding. The work was finished in a month. I originally thought of the shed as a place to keep a spare set of clothes, or where I could shower if I had been running on the trails. But one evening before I moved into Le Conte, I was sitting with my design assistant, Samantha, on Adirondack chairs outside the shed's tiny door, and I said, "I don't know if I want to move into that big house. I'm so at home here."

Now the Shed would become my home. More than that, the Shed was where I began an emotional and spiritual detox for my soul. It had been the first thing I built by myself after the divorce, and my first attempt to restore some of the confidence that had been decimated. I came to understand that my tiny house was the place for me to rediscover what I truly meant by the word *home.* I had to walk away from almost every single thing that had been my life. I had to leave behind most of the trappings of my exterior life, including a 10,000-square-foot house, as well as clothes, coats, shoes. The only companion who could join me was my dog, Buddy.

When there is nothing to fix or clean, nowhere to host, entertain, or cook, life has no choice but to bend toward simplicity.

The smallness of the space offered a chance for my soul to breathe.

After living in so many homes, placing myself inside 360 square feet left me nowhere to hide from an unexamined life. I could not distract myself by walking into another room, by rearranging furniture or organizing a pantry. It was a humbling experience; I had to let go, to quit trying to fix things, and cede control over my day and my world. I also had to depend one hundred percent on Blackberry Farm, and that was a challenge for me. Being in the hospitality business had made me far more comfortable giving than receiving, and it was a humbling privilege to be "mothered" so perfectly by the place I had helped begin. After the divorce, Sam had told me, "Mom, you know Blackberry will always take care of you." At the time, I wanted him to say, "Mom, you know *I* will always take care of you." But I realize now that Sam knew he and I unconditionally loved the same place, and were loved unconditionally in return.

My first lesson in the Shed was to truly learn the gift of receiving. If I wanted to eat, I had to wander into one of the restaurant kitchens or dining rooms. I had to enjoy someone else's menu around someone else's time. I had to feel gratitude for what they made me. I think that the day-to-day rhythm and the practice of receiving are what prepared me to really receive God and to listen to that little voice inside of me. I had to declare the fight over and surrender. By the light of a single lamp, I had to meet my true self head-on.

I had a lot of time to do it, too. I can tell you about sleeping after a divorce. There isn't much of it. It was hard to fall asleep, and I could not wait to get up in the morning. I was restless. I would get up in the dark, drink coffee, do devotionals, pray, and think.

I also came to discover that I not only owned my own time— physically, mentally, and emotionally—but I also was owed my own time and I needed to spend it on fixing myself. If I wanted to be healed, if I wanted to become a better person, I had to put in the hours, not just on Sundays at church, but every day. I couldn't distract myself with chores or entertaining someone else. It was just me, Buddy, and God.

For the first time in my life during those months, I was the project, the remodel, the thing to be cleared out. The process was joyful; it was the path I could take to becoming a more whole and more compassionate human being. Every morning, I was overcome with the feeling of being known for the first time.

Inside those walls, I read, I prayed, and I listened in a way that I had never done before. Previously, when I was confronted with a problem at work or in life, I went home and worked on it. Now I prayed about it. I prayed for guidance, I prayed for understanding. It was not as if a solution or a resolution miraculously appeared. Rather, it was that I developed a different focus, away from control and toward acceptance. I stopped seeing my life as something completely novel and unique and started seeing all the ways that my experiences paralleled the lives of people in the Bible two thousand years ago. My problems were not all that different from their problems. We all take turns being lepers, we all will be the person lying desperate by the side of the road, we all have the opportunity to be the good Samaritan. The same way that they had needed God's guidance and strength, I needed God's guidance and strength. He had always been there—I just didn't know it. But now I was learning. In the silence and the solitude, He was there.

One of my favorite Bible stories in the Book of Luke recounts how Jesus came to dine with two sisters, Mary and Martha. Martha opens her home to Jesus, but after he enters, she busies herself in the kitchen, "distracted by all the preparations," as Luke says. I envision her bent over a hot fire, sweating as she works, sweeping the stray charcoal bits, wiping her hands on her apron as she serves the plates. All the while, her sister, Mary, sits at Jesus's feet, listening to him speak and preach. Two sides of the same hospitality coin.

One thing I have come to love about the Bible is how much is left to our imaginations to fill in. The stories are drawn with such a broad brush that they can be imagined in a kitchen in Tennessee, Alabama, Georgia, or South Carolina. I can hear Martha, exasperated, as she asks Jesus why he does not care that Mary has left her with all the work, and then, without waiting for an answer, she adds, "Tell her to help me!" But Jesus replies that while Martha is upset about many things, few things are needed. Mary has chosen not to immerse herself in busyness, but rather to stop, to listen, to devote her full attention to Jesus. She has decided to be present. As Jesus says, Mary has chosen the thing that is needed, the thing that cannot be taken away.

I see myself so clearly in Martha. I have always been the busy woman in the kitchen, hands full, juggling bowls, mixers, chef's knives, and spoons, watching the stove, fussing over my table.

What Jesus was trying to tell Martha, and what I think he is trying to tell me, is that what matters is not how clean my kitchen looks or how impressive my food is. It's not about how busy I can make myself or how many tasks I can complete. What really matters is being present. I do not need to have the most lavish table; I need to take the time to know the people who have come to my table, to stop and listen. Make everyone part of what you create.

In the quiet of the Shed, at night, I had learned to sit like Mary. I had learned to listen. Now I needed to do that with people.

Chapter 26

INSIDE OUT

In the beginning, even after the divorce, one person I couldn't shed was Sandy. We met for lunch every three or four weeks. We occasionally went to Doug's church—in fact, Sandy was there when Doug delivered a sermon about his friend "Mary," whose life had been pruned by a divorce that she did not want. We tried to keep up the appearance of normalcy, as if to say, "See, it's no big deal, we all get along, everything looks fine so it must be fine." We went to little Sam's football games, and in April 2013, a year after our divorce became final, we went to Grandparents' Day at the grandkids' school, which was actually two back-to-back days of events, three hours each day, together.

Sandy likes to be the first to arrive and the first to leave. He always gets an aisle seat and always has an exit strategy. In the auditorium, he had saved one for me. Then we went to each classroom and the cafeteria for lunch. On the second day, I arrived and saw him already seated. He was wearing a tailored, high-fashion leather coat and underneath, a striped Eton shirt. Each shirt button was a different color and the buttonholes were sewn in different colored thread. In a year, he had gone from a regular guy in khaki pants and white button-downs to an urban chic dresser. It was a visual awakening for me. He looked as if he were walking down a very different path. And inside my head, I heard a voice saying, *Stop it, Kreis. Stop torturing yourself.*

The next day, I called and canceled our upcoming lunch. I never rescheduled. I told myself, *Wherever he is, you must not go there. You will never be able to start over if you keep revisiting the past.* That clean break was when my healing finally began.

Around Knoxville, behind my back, I knew people probably talked about the dissolution of our marriage. With genuine kindness, both of Sandy's parents reached out to me, and kept in regular touch. My parents, who were deep in their own problems with my father becoming more difficult and demanding each year, preferred to say nothing. I didn't blame them, they belonged to a generation that was uncomfortable with divorce, and they didn't want to say the wrong thing. The only people who commented were old friends, who would tell me they couldn't believe it, that Sandy and I seemed unshakable. They would tell me that we seemed so devoted to each other, so loyal, such best friends. Sometimes those words comforted me and other times they would remind me just how gutted I felt. I still couldn't absorb the shock.

Outside of my family and friends, I felt as if I had unwittingly donned Harry Potter's invisibility cloak. My married friends had no idea what to do with single people, in particular with a once but no longer married woman. Divorced and widowed women are the odd place setting, the extra chair, the thing that throws off a room's tidy symmetry. Friends would preface an invitation with the words "Would you feel weird if . . ." or excuse a non-invite by saying, "We didn't want you to feel weird . . ." Either way, I felt weird. And I felt lonely.

Making new friends was difficult. Most people who didn't know me thought of me as "not approachable." They saw me through the lens of my Blackberry reputation and glossy magazine photos. The divorce only added fuel to the unapproachable fire. I was like a leper—people kept a wide berth and left me alone. I remember sitting by myself at a bridal luncheon in New York City for Dee's daughter, Whitney. A woman I knew slightly and who had her own investment management company in Knoxville, walked over and said, "Hey, can I sit down?" We talked all through lunch, and that one gesture became the cornerstone of a deep friendship. My now good friend, Sharon Pryse, doesn't judge, she genuinely likes people. And she was a little like me, in that she knew tons of people but, as she said, most of her relationships have been based around work. Sharon also loves to travel, so when I was going to New York on business, she came. She's one of my few friends who likes the Ashram and will go with me. Most people visit once and say, "I'm never doing that again."

As the months passed, I was "fixed up" with other single women outside of my existing Knoxville constellation. We had coffee or met for dinners. Some were divorced, a few were bitter, others were widows, like Brenda Wood. She and I found so much to share that we quickly set up a standing dinner date. But I still had work to do on myself. I couldn't be vulnerable just inside the walls of the Shed. I had to be willing to be imperfect and vulnerable out in the larger world.

I continued going to Bible study, and for two years, Doug had chided me to see a counselor. I kept putting him off, saying I was too busy working at Blackberry, I didn't need it. Counseling couldn't do anything. But life in the quiet of the Shed had freed up a considerable amount of my time. I was running out of excuses. A woman I knew recommended Teresa, a Christian counselor, and I finally agreed.

Counseling was not what I had expected. Teresa was direct and straightforward. She didn't equivocate or spend each hour probing my feelings. Instead, she pushed me to be introspective about my actions. She would ask a question. Then she would ask a follow-up. She wanted me to think about my choices and my responses. She didn't want me to answer yes before she had asked the question. She wanted me to take responsibility for my answers and for my life.

This push towards self-knowledge came at a very interesting time. I had been invited to give a speech at the Antiques and Garden Show of Nashville. Suzanne Kasler and I were being paired to talk about what I assumed was design.

It was typical Kreis: answer yes and then ask, *what is the question?* I went to Nashville to meet with the organizers and ask what they wanted me to talk about. Their reply was "Whatever you want." I asked for a little bit of direction, as if they were a design client. In design, the most difficult situations are when someone says "Just do what you want" and then once you've done it, the client doesn't like it. But their answer was "No, really, we want you to talk about whatever you want." I decided that the only reason I had been invited was because of Blackberry, so I would just give them my Blackberry story.

But when I finished the first draft, it read like the punch list of everything I'd done for the last forty years at Blackberry. It was boring, and it wasn't my story. It might have been my story seventeen years before, or even five years or five months ago, but not now. When I went into the Shed, I gave up my exit strategy.

I could no longer run away to the next room, let alone to a weekend house or vacation spot. I was no longer constantly packing or unpacking. I was not methodically working my way through a sink full of dishes. I was not dividing plants or rolling piecrust or arranging cuttings from the garden.

I have a friend who says, "Don't live your 'shoulds,'" and for forty years, I had been living my shoulds: *Should I have so and so over? Should I go wash my clothes? Should I tidy up the house? Should I plan something for tomorrow? Should I go work on the roses? Should I do anything?* In the Shed, there were no shoulds. It was a huge unburdening. I shook myself of busyness and stepped off the hamster wheel. Full stop. At dusk, when I came through the door with Buddy, I had to greet silence and solitude. The way I had oriented the windows, I couldn't even see a stray golf cart, walker, or any other vehicle pass by on the road. And I couldn't hear them, either. I was fully alone. Slowly, night after night, I read books like *The Wisdom of Stability* by Jonathan Wilson-Hartgrove and Sue Monk Kidd's *When the Heart Waits,* and as if from a very old chrysalis, my own story emerged.

It was not always a pretty story. There had been loss and sadness. There had been single-mindedness and self-centeredness, some of which would take me far longer than a half a year in a shed to overcome. There were regrets and absences. There was the recurring question of "Where was I?" I had almost always been physically present, but so often my mind, my heart, and my spirit had been focused more on the places I was maintaining than on the people in front of me. Even something as simple as holding my children's hands: Did I not take Sam's hand because he was not a hand-holder, or because my own hands were always occupied? Once I began to acknowledge my truths, there was no going back. I could no longer fake a pleasant presentation, I couldn't do simply what was expected. For the first time in nearly sixty-two years, I had to tell my story.

So I began to think, what do I know? What is the one thing I really want to talk about? The answer was simple: home. Everything in my life, whether it was cooking, gardening, work, Blackberry, moving, entertaining, friends, or family, everything had been centered around home. My talk was about home. Yet it had taken moving to a shed to really understand that while home is what had always mattered most to me, a house is not a home. The true meaning of home is much deeper.

I began by writing the story of the houses that had mattered most, and over the course of several months, the talk that I ended up with was very different from the one I had planned when I first said yes. I wrote about the start of Blackberry and the call from my mother to take a cooking class, about Rose Bay and the fire, and Maple Cottage and my accident. Then I moved to something bigger than walls and windows. I wrote, "For me, it is easy to build buildings. But now I am going to share something that is extremely more difficult to build than buildings, and that is self-confidence." I talked about living life without seventy percent of my hearing. I told about my divorce. And I wrote about my relationship with God. "My pastor had prayed for ten years after my accident that I might know God. And in the midst of my pain, I clung to faith, to a God who is never going to leave me. It is faith in God that has renewed the joy that was hard to feel after my divorce. He has given me the people who have encouraged me, who have prayed for me when I was hurting, and who have surrounded me with more love than I could ever hope to repay. It is so important to have companions along the way, people to encourage you on the journey," I said, adding, "Find those people in your life. None of us are meant to walk this life alone."

I decided instead of showing photos of comfortable guest rooms and palette-pleasing interiors on the big screen behind me, I wanted to show photos of my family and of the team at Blackberry, the people who make the dream of Blackberry come to life every day. For years, I had given so much to Blackberry, not just time and effort, but the proceeds of my salary by never getting paid, the furniture from my house, art, whatever was needed. When I moved in to the Shed, Blackberry had given it all back and more. But it had not chosen to repay me with things. Rather, it had been the place to care for and nurture me.

To end the talk, I wrote, "My life has been full of sorrow, but a lot more joy. Hard things will happen. You will be disappointed, but the key is to look at it square in the eye, deal with it, move on, and keep dreaming. My story of Blackberry Farm at the end of the day is a love story. I believe that a home can heal, it can restore, and like Dorothy said, 'There's no place like home.'

"It's all the things that we can't get our hands on that end up being the most important in life. I am so happy to know that God has me in the palm of His hand. For me, God is home. Hold on to whatever your home is for you." I ended with my new favorite aphorism:

All it takes is all you've got.
And it is worth it.

The talk was finished, but I was nervous. I was sure Suzanne wouldn't like it. I went to Atlanta and had a friend who had helped to edit it read it aloud to Suzanne. "Don't do it," she told me. It was way too personal; it needed to be more professional. I replied that I knew that, but it was also my story. She suggested that I change it, there was still plenty of time. I answered, "I'll think about it."

I tried to rewrite it to make it neutral. I'd work on it and then read what I'd done to my design assistant, Samantha. Each time, she'd say, "Nah, I like the old one better."

And it was true. I had always defined myself as "Yes, I'm Kreis Beall." I had never asked myself, "But, who are you?" Once I began to answer that question, once I told myself my story, I couldn't go back to the first script.

HOW I LEARNED TO PRAY

Each person's prayer is different; each person has their own way to pray. For me to really pray, I have to be totally alone. In the Bible, Matthew 6:6 speaks to me: "But when you pray, go into your room, close the door and pray to your Father, who is unseen. Then your Father, who sees what is done in secret, will reward you." Perhaps for this reason, I find it hard to pray out loud. Indeed, I'm not sure that I have ever really "learned" to pray, as in having a formula or a skill. My best guide in many ways was a woman I never met, Sue Monk Kidd. I read her book When the Heart Waits *while I was waiting in the Shed. She writes about the need to make a chrysalis, to stop, and go inside yourself to search for meaning and what matters. She taught me to build my own chrysalis, go inside, and be comfortable in the silence. Accept that I needed to wait, without knowing any of the answers, without being able to see the larger plan. I had to take it on faith that I would reemerge from my chrysalis. And I did.*

Today, I still pray in much the same way as I began in the Shed. I simply talk to God, most often in the very early morning, in the dark, by being still. Prayer for me is also a feeling. It is a feeling of slowing down to write or speak. It is in that act of slowing down that I am drawn into a deeper life, one that flows below the surface of my busy days.

When I lived in the Shed, inspired by Sue Monk Kidd, I wrote these notes to myself about the power of prayer: There are no books about the process of waiting, no classes on how to wait. Instead there is simply turning yourself upside down, emptying out, and letting God refill you. Amen.

Chapter 27

MAKING A SPLASH IN NASHVILLE

I knew enough to realize that I didn't know the first thing about giving a speech. I asked Doug for guidance, and he told me to listen to Apple Computer founder Steve Jobs's Stanford University commencement speech. A friend gave me the book *Talk Like TED* and told me to watch TED Talks. So I listened to Steve Jobs and others, and I learned that whatever the topic, the entire story had to be told in about eighteen minutes, and that I needed to practice. But on January 31, 2015, as I sat backstage in the Nashville Music City Center, I felt the sweat pool inside my black dress, which I had carefully chosen for the occasion on the theory that black is the color least likely to show perspiration. Fortunately my shoes were black because I could feel my feet sweating, too.

The actress Diane Keaton had been the Antiques and Garden Show's keynote speaker the day before, and now, after passing through display areas packed with beautiful antiques, fine art, artisan jewelry, and lush garden installations, some seven hundred women and men were gathering to listen to Suzanne Kasler and me. Suzanne was speaking first—her talk was entitled "Design at Blackberry Farm," and mine was called "The Passion of Design." I went back and forth on the title, and later realized it should have been called "The Passion of Home," but like so much else in life, it was too late to make a change.

Secluded away behind the curtains, we could hear the scrape of the chairs and the buzz of small talk and a few laughs. I decided now might be an excellent time to start praying. As my own personal joke about my hearing deficit and the way I conflated words and sounds, I had started calling God Howie— short for Howard, as in Howard (rather than Hallowed) Be Thy Name. I was starting to pray to Howie when we walked out. The light was stronger than I had remembered and the antiseptic space was suddenly animated by holding so many people. On the stage was a couch, a low table, a plant, and a podium, with a large screen hanging behind. As I adjusted my legs against the couch cushions, my mind wandered. I thought of my granddaughters playing ballerina in gauzy pink skirts or the little girls who would come to my short-lived children's photography studio. Around a camera, they were sometimes shy and scared, until they saw the tutus. There was something about putting on that mesh skirt that transformed them. They would twirl and jump and spin and rise up on their toes, becoming the happiest and freest version of themselves. The last thing I did before I started speaking was ask God to give me a tutu.

I began with the obvious: How am I supposed to follow Suzanne Kasler and Diane Keaton? "There is absolutely nothing in the world that I can up Suzanne Kasler on, but with Diane, there is just one little thing. I heard Diane say that she has lived in thirty houses. Well, I have lived in forty. I'm a house junkie, too." Then I asked everyone to stand up and do a yoga mountain pose and a chair pose. After that, I began. As the words came out, I felt like I was finally exhaling. I was opening up myself. When I finished, every person in that room was on their feet. Some were laughing, and many were wiping away tears.

Later a woman approached me and said, "I truly thought that you were going to get up there and tell me whether I should paint my room blue or pink." People I had never met said, "Thank you for being honest."

Among all the aphorisms I have collected, perhaps the most lasting is just these three sentences from Sheryl Louise Moller: "Tell the truth. Tell the truth. Tell the truth." I often wonder why I avoided speaking honestly for years, and the best analogy I can think of is a horse that runs back into a burning barn. There is a fire, it's hot, it's deadly, but the horse runs back because it's what he knows. The only way to pull the animal to safety is to cover its head and lead it away. All those years, I didn't have anyone to cover my head, put a rope around me, and say "Come to this pasture. It's not what you planned, it's not what you expected, but it's filled with possibilities." Instead, I just kept running back into that burning barn.

If there's one thing that I can accomplish in my life now, it's throwing a lifeline to someone else in need. I've been the person who needed that help, and I've also been the negligent bystander, the one who walked by the fire or the one who thought, *Why can't that person just pick up their mat and take care of themselves? Why can't they work harder? Why can't they just deal with their problem?* I know now that it is never that simple. There is a reason why it says in Galatians 6:2, "Bear one another's burdens and so fulfill the law of Christ."

In the course of stumbling around for guidance with my own talk, I came across the Harry Potter author J. K. Rowling's address to the 2008 graduating class at Harvard University. Most of the speech is about the benefits of failure. She talks about how failure gave her an inner security and taught her about herself. Only when she was broken did she discover her own strong will and discipline. Only then did she find she had friends "whose value was truly above the price of rubies." I recognized all of those sentiments, and one more line: when she talked about hitting rock bottom, being as close to homelessness as it was possible to be in Great Britain. She said, "And so rock bottom became the solid foundation on which I rebuilt my life."

Rock bottom was also where I began to rebuild my life. And the rock that met me at the bottom was God. God was what had told me, Pick yourself up from your despair, go do something, go be something, go share something, go think of something for someone else. Be lonely, be still, because when you have been lonely and still, you will learn how to go and sit next to someone else who is also lonely and still. Be hurt, because then you can feel compassion for the stranger in line behind you who is also hurting. Be small, because it is the small kindnesses that move the world. Be mindful, because each first light, each walk, each thank-you, each smile, matters. Be joyful, because it is far better to find goodness than to find fault. And on days when none of that works, just be, because the next day or the day after that may be your chance to be grateful, to know thoughtfulness, to see love, to be needed, to be surprised, or simply to begin again in the world.

By the time I gave my Nashville speech, I had left the Shed and moved in to the old farmhouse diagonally across the narrow roadway, newly renovated and newly renamed Hedgerose. Each morning I could look out from my kitchen window and see exactly where I had been. When the world grew too fast or loud, or I found myself falling back into old patterns, all I had to do was take my key, walk across the road, and open the Shed's door. I could sit inside and think, I could spend the night in a small space, I could sit in a silence that I had chosen and make space for God to come in.

Outside, I was finding a community of friends and of faith. I had even started to pick up some of my discarded shoulds, but these were very different from my previous sense of obligations. I decided I should spend special time with each of my grand-children, and I would start with Cameron, who was close to leaving home for college. I decided that I should travel. I decided I should host more family events, and I started having Monday-night family dinners for whoever could come, for Sam and Mary Celeste and their kids. And I decided that I should do more to be present in the lives of my sons.

Chapter 28

FRIDAYS WITH SAM

Thirty-six years after Sam and I first got to know each other in the kitchen at Blackberry, we started to become reacquainted in the dining room. In typical Sam fashion, it began with a quick, direct sentence, "Mom, let's have lunch every week." I said yes, and he picked Fridays at noon.

It wasn't going to be every Friday—sometimes he was out of town, sometimes I was—but any Friday when we were both there, we met for lunch. It was always at Blackberry, always in the original dining room, the wood-paneled space with the big bay window, and we always sat at the same table, table sixty-one, tucked in the left-hand corner, with a banquette. Whenever I arrived, the hostess would ask, "Do you want to go to sixty-one?" and I'd answer yes. I always sat facing out into the room and Sam always sat turned in, facing me and the wall. That way he wouldn't be distracted by trying to subtly assess the service, the guests, and the tables turning, by noticing when the bread baskets arrived and whose meals came out in what order, and how often the busboys refilled the water. With his back to the room, it was also unlikely that guests would recognize him.

Most Fridays, I was there before Sam because I didn't have people waiting in line to see me. But Sam always left time for our hour together. Early on, he came equipped with a list of things to ask, each topic written out on a notepad. It was awkward and formal; there was no casual chitchat. But it was also the first time the two of us had been together, just us, in any sustained way since he had left for college at eighteen, half of his lifetime ago. He was now a father with four children, and in another year, he and Mary Celeste would have a fifth baby. He was a competitive cyclist. He ran a business with close to four hundred employees, me being one of them. Under him, Blackberry had won *Travel and Leisure*'s award for "Best in the World in Service," and tens of other accolades. He had held Blackberry together when the 2008 financial crash decimated many other destinations.

Being back at Blackberry, I got to see him through his team members' eyes, particularly because I was one of those team members. He'd bike first thing in the morning and come straight to his office, grubby and still in his gear, carrying a big bowl of healthy food to eat. He'd listen to whatever issue was being presented as he ate. Sam said very little in meetings. He wanted everybody to put their facts on the table, and then he would absorb what had been said and reach a decision. It was inclusive of everyone, using such a different process from the way Sandy and I had done things. We had been far more likely to argue over an issue or simply make a snap decision on the spot, with one or two other people involved, rather than involving a full team and having a wide-ranging discussion.

The next time I'd see Sam during the day, he was showered

and dressed to greet guests. He worked the floor of the farm's restaurants for years. He could stop and have a conversation with a guest for twenty-five minutes, making that person feel like the center of the Blackberry universe, even when he had a long list of things to do. He had incredible patience for anyone who came to Blackberry. But appreciating all of this and seeing what he had accomplished didn't give us a relationship. It had been years since Sam had needed a mom to keep his snack drawer filled.

No matter whether there are true or false hurts in a relationship, if something is missing, if there is an awkwardness on one or both sides, it is difficult to know how to make it right. I could have all kinds of internal dialogues in my head and envision how Sam and I would hug each other hello and sit down and talk about how lucky we were, talk about his children, about our family, about Blackberry, about the future, and then tell happy stories about the past. But that's not how it worked. In our relationship, neither Sam nor I was a great emotional communicator. We weren't nostalgic reminiscers. So week after week, we simply showed up for lunch and talked business, almost like two strangers. Instead of truly talking, we tried letting our actions speak what our hearts and mouths could not.

But like most things that are repeated over and over, our lunches became more relaxed. After about two years of agendas and to-be-discusseds, one Friday Sam looked up at me with those strong blue eyes, and said, "I want to know you, Mom."

I never said, "Why did you finally ask me this now?" Looking back, I wish I had. I wish Sam and I had that sort of casual, matter-of-fact relationship where I could have said, "Well, this is where I've been all these years—where have you been?" But when Sam followed that up by asking, "What's important to you?" I answered, "God, family, and friends," and then I asked, "What's important to you?"

"My family," he replied, pausing and saying it in that perfect, economical Sam way. "Taking care of my chicks." He told me how he had decided to make it a personal rule that he was not going to stay in the kitchen or dining room at Blackberry past eight or nine each evening so he could go home and cook dinner for his children, even if he started cooking at nine p.m. He insisted on making morning pancakes, too. The Webb School must have needed an entire order of tardy slips just for the Beall clan. But Sam knew that Cameron was only a few years away from leaving for college, and every moment was fleeting and precious. He was going to put his family first.

So much time had passed and I'd never really talked to my own son about emotions or spiritual life or anything that mattered except grandchildren. Even then, it was often more of a catch-up on activities, school, and issues rather than a deeper talk about who they were as people and the ways that they were growing and who they were becoming. And although Sam and I were finally talking, the conversations were still punctuated by business. We couldn't escape the office, especially not when we were eating in the office's dining room. So after a few more lunches, I asked Sam if he'd come with me to Teresa Dunn, my counselor. I thought it might help to have someone who could act as a bit of a mediator and keep the conversation going. To my surprise, he agreed.

I met with Teresa on Tuesdays, which was the worst day for anyone who ran Blackberry. Tuesday was set aside for meetings and reviews. But Sam came. He couldn't come every week, but we settled into an uneven pattern of him heading into Knoxville.

What I remember most from the sessions was Sam asking, "I really want to know what happened. Growing up, you were supermom—there wasn't anything you couldn't or didn't do. What happened?"

I had never considered myself from Sam's perspective: going from supermom to the wounded mom that nobody knew what to do with, particularly Sam. At last, with Teresa's help, we started to talk about the accident. I said that the first thing I wanted him to know was that I'd never been bitter, never wondered why me, never felt that anyone, especially Sam, was in any way responsible. It was an accident. In the classic dictionary definition, it was something unforeseen, unplanned, and unintended. If I had landed two or three inches back on the dirt or grass, likely everything would have been different.

I told him that the chipping away of "supermom" came from the deafness, that it had taken me several years to absorb its full effects and to lose my self-confidence. I told him how I hadn't understood that losing my identity at Blackberry would be so significant, too. I tried to shift my fulfillment into sustaining my marriage, but then my marriage was unable to survive the people Sandy and I became. By the time I lost my health, my work, and my husband, my self-confidence was completely shattered. So I did something I should have done years before: I turned to God. Walking God's path was the way I had started to find a new fulfillment and a new kind of joy.

I'm grateful to have had that conversation, to have been able to tell him that the change in me was the cumulative impact of so many of my choices. And I'm grateful I let him know how proud I was that he had already realized that work isn't everything.

I know if someone had asked me at age thirty-eight or thirty-nine what mattered most, I would not necessarily have said "my chicks." I would have probably said Blackberry first. I can remember years when we lived in Mobile and I couldn't wait until Sandy went out of town because it meant I could work later. I would start a project at six or seven p.m., after the boys had eaten, and I'd be up until midnight or later. I was a great calendar mom, with lots of special events and jam-packed weekends. I made sure that when Sandy traveled, I was at home with the boys, and vice versa, so we never had to leave them with babysitters, but I wasn't a wrap-my-arms-around-my-sons, comfort-their-hurts, and ask-them-about-their-day type of mom. I didn't know how, and I didn't try to learn.

Sam wanted his home to be different. He took the physical world of the houses he loved growing up in and then changed the dynamic inside the walls. He always wanted to live in one place, in one house. He wanted roots. He married a woman, Mary Celeste, who is a wrap-your-arms-around-your-child mom. He nurtured her so she could nurture the family they built together. He was intentional in how he went about his life, from the smallest thing like not wanting a microwave—although he never saw that as small—to putting his family above everything else. Once, I asked him, "When did you finally become comfortable in your own skin?" Without hesitation, he said, "When I became a husband and a father."

In those meetings with Teresa, while Sam got to know me, I also got to see more deeply into Sam. He had grown up around two parents who filled up a room, his father especially, but his mother, too. Sam was different. He was never the splash—he might even be overlooked at first because he was so quiet. But Sam never overlooked anything. He constantly observed and evaluated, and then he would determine his own course and carry out his own plan. He didn't want to be the actor under the lights and on the stage; he wanted to be the director behind the scenes. He said very little, but when he spoke, everyone grew quiet and listened. Even with me, he said so much just by asking his question. He saw his mother, still deaf, still divorced, still by herself, yet finding meaning in life. How did this happen? He wanted to know. Who is she? How has she decided what matters? How had she found God in her life?

A few times, I went with Sam, Mary Celeste, and their children to their church, Cedar Springs Presbyterian in West Knoxville. Cedar Springs had the same wonderful pastor for decades, Pastor John Wood, but Doug often served as the guest preacher when Pastor Wood was out of town. One Sunday after Doug had preached, as we were walking to pick up the kids from Sunday school, Sam asked, "Mom, that's your pastor, right?" I said yes, and all Sam said in reply was "Well, I like him, too."

A few years later, Doug would tell the story of how Sam had called him and asked to talk. He told Doug that his wife had "fallen in love with another man, Jesus Christ," and he wanted to know something about this guy. He saw so many women in his life, his mother, his wife, even his oldest daughter, Cameron, finding faith. After Doug finished giving his explanation, Sam looked at him and said, "How do you know this is true?" Doug recounted he felt like this had been his least successful pastoral meeting ever. But Sam's approach was the opposite of my "The answer's yes—what's the question?" To him, the question *was* what mattered. To ask meant that something or someone was deserving of his time. What matters to you? What happened? Or as it says in Matthew, "Ask, and it will be given to you. Seek, and you shall find."

Sam and I had about ten hours in total with Teresa. Not

enough to reset a relationship, but enough to make it deeper and to make repairs. By meeting each other as adults in this way, we were both able to see the fully formed people we had become. We uncovered each other's complexities. We discovered that we liked each other. Sam usually came with a list of questions: why this, what's that? And I got a do-over. Finally, his mother was not going to be too busy or too distracted or too rushed. I was going to thoughtfully answer each and every one. I wanted to exhaust his list before I got to mine. We thought now that we were talking, there was going to be plenty of time.

Chapter 29

A SEASON OF FRIENDSHIP

A very well-meaning friend told me, "Look, I don't know if anyone is going to want to date you. You're a hard one. The problem is, you're intimidating to most men." I was considered "unapproachable," and as for me doing the approaching, I truly had no idea where to begin.

And if starting to date at sixty is hard, it's a lot more complicated with a disability.

Yet when I finally did have my first date, I was overcome with the same giddy butterflies-in-the-stomach sensation that I remembered from four decades ago. The extra time fussing at the mirror, scouring my closet for what to wear, nerves and possibilities braided together end over end like my granddaughter Josephine's flaxen hair.

I planned the outlines of the evening in meticulous detail. I chose a weeknight, and I picked the most familiar spot possible, a specific table in the Barn at Blackberry. I would be discreetly surrounded by people I knew. I wouldn't have to worry about what to order; I already knew my way to the ladies' room. And

I would be able to hear. I purposely choose a quiet night when the restaurant wouldn't be noisy and the hostess thoughtfully seated us so that my left ear was closest to him. The wine bottle had been presented and the first glass poured when I looked at my handsome date in his tie, pressed shirt, and navy blue jacket, who spoke in a low-toned voice that was, for me, so easy to hear, and asked, "How old are you?"

"Fifty," he answered. So I asked, "Fifty what? Fifty-two, fifty-four?"

"Just fifty," he replied.

I told him I was sixty, and all he said was "Is that a problem?"

Was it a problem? How would I even define a problem in a relationship? Midlife dating is littered with people, men and women, who have built unbreachable walls, who are stuck in old patterns, who refuse to grow up, or who have been unfaithful, and yet you must take on faith that this time something has changed. We have an appetizer and an entrée to present our best selves, which invariably need soft lighting to smooth out the fine lines and slackening chins.

I took to naming my dates, just as I had named my houses, although I had far fewer dates than homes. My fifty-year-old I dubbed Turtle, because he turned out to have a hard, impenetrable shell. He would periodically emerge, with his tanned face and flash a boyish smile, but the only vulnerability he ever showed began and ended that first evening. He was a brief but reliable texter, a few quick bubbles of conversation and then he was gone, the modern-day equivalent of those high school boys who tapped the brake as they passed a girl and gave a quick wave or cute shout-out with the window rolled down.

The next man I nicknamed Harley Boy. We had gone to high school together and dated for about a minute when we were both sixteen. I hadn't seen him since he visited me one time at Tulane. He had been a motorcycle rider back then, and true to form, he arrived for our first date astride a gleaming Harley-Davidson. His icy blue eyes were just as I remembered them. I hopped on and we rode for three hours through the dips and curves of the Smoky Mountains. We hiked, picnicked, and slow-danced outside under the stars. Everyone looks better under stars.

We never made any serious plans, and I was happy watching football, eating pizza, drinking beer, and sitting for hours by the fire, but Harley Boy was happier still to play the field. One of the luxuries of turning sixty is that there is no need to waste time on high school relationship theatrics so when he moved to Florida, I waved goodbye and he and his Harley were gone. But I also wasn't focused on dating and men. Instead, I had discovered a newfound joy in female friendships.

The last time I had had any significant relationships outside of work had been during our years in Alabama where we were linked together through kids and family life. I knew wonderful women, but we all lived our lives in various stages of a whirlwind. Now with my children grown and largely unencumbered, I finally had the time to devote to friendship.

My season in the Shed had been my chrysalis, the cocoon that had held me together and kept me safe while I morphed into my new self. Now the wounds were largely healed. Hedgerose's renovation was complete and I was splitting my time between Blackberry and the River Cottage, a house I had rented in Knoxville. When I wasn't home, I was traveling. I started the year in Paris with my granddaughter Cameron and by December, I had been everywhere from California, to New York, Miami, and even completed a three-thousand-mile drive to Maine with two friends. Along the way, we laughed, we read books, we shared.

When I was home, my house was full. Whether it was with my sorority of granddaughters, or groups of friends cooking dinner, there was always life in my rooms. I was asked to do a series of cooking schools at a friend's house; it had been nearly twenty years since I had last led a cooking school. I hosted a women's Bible study with a group that ranged in age from twenty-two to eighty-eight. On the wall of my dining room, I hung the family portrait that had been painted in Hilton Head all those years ago. The portrait had been wrapped and stored in a crate for years until Sandy and I affixed it to a wall in our last Alabama house. When I was unboxing our accumulated things, I looked at it and saw a pretty painting with bright, hopeful colors. I thought, *I can put this up again, I'll just remove Sandy.* And that's what I did. I asked an artist to cut and reframe the canvas. To me it signified my new start.

I was finally present in my own life, living in the moment and sharing the moment with my family and my ever-widening circle of friends.

In October, I was having dinner at Sam and Mary Celeste's, and Sam said, "I want to tell you something."

We didn't stand and talk in the kitchen or back by the grill; instead Sam led me to the porch, where we could be alone. Sandy was getting remarried, and Sam wanted me to hear it from him first. The same woman whose name I had seen on Sandy's cell phone three years ago was now becoming his wife.

The wedding took place about ten days later. In a sign of how much our entire world has changed, a few of my girlfriends broke the news to me after seeing photos of the Tom Ford wedding dress and the ring on Instagram.

I received a flurry of texts and calls from friends worried about me, but news that might have been devastating two years ago was now tolerable. By providing clarity, it was even strangely freeing. It provided a form of closure. Rather than spending more years living under the shadow of that question *Is this all there is?* Sandy had found his path. I was finding mine. We would always be bound by our sons, our daughters-in-law, and our grandchildren, but we did not have to be bound together to love our family. I rang in the New Year with Camille and her family in Alabama and was making plans for 2016.

On February 24, Sam hosted a family dinner and birthday celebration for Mary Anne Beall. It was a night of food, laughter, and joy. We wore shiny magenta party hats. While all the grandkids and Mary Celeste and Mary Anne and I were clustered at one end, Sam sat and talked to his grandfather for more than thirty minutes about the ways he wanted to grow Blackberry so that there was something of it that would appeal to each of his children.

It was happy. We were happy. I didn't know that the next morning Sam was catching a pre-dawn flight bound for the snowy slopes of Beaver Creek, Colorado, and a weekend of skiing with friends.

MAKING SOMEONE COMFORTABLE

For years, I thought that making someone comfortable was all physical space and physical comfort. And that does matter. After designing hundreds of Blackberry guest rooms, I learned to pay attention to every detail when I had someone stay in my home. I wanted to make sure that in my guest room, I leave an empty closet or some empty drawers for guests to put their things away. I would have fresh towels, toiletries, soft sheets, a TV, and plugs and chargers within easy reach. I make sure to share the WiFi password, have new magazines, perhaps a book, as well as fresh flowers or a bit of fruit and a bottle of water on the nightstand. I let guests know how to adjust the heat or the air-conditioning. Most of all, I want to create a space that they could make their own while they stayed, down to knowing how to get their own coffee or tea in the morning.

But sometimes welcoming and making another person comfortable requires doing more. It is noticing if an older person needs a raised chair with arms because it has become harder for them to get up and down from a soft, low chair. It is noticing if a parent needs a break or if a child needs a fun distraction after sitting too long. It can even be acknowledging what I call the elephant in the room. I remember one of my friends, Betsey Bush. She wasn't a close friend—we served on some committees together, but her son was married to Sharon Pryse's stepdaughter, and in the way of how Southern things still go, it's a connection. My friend Brenda and I learned that Betsey had been diagnosed with terminal bone cancer and given three months to live. And so we asked her to come to dinner with us at Ruth's Chris Steak House, because we knew she liked it. After we picked her up, I asked her flat out, "So, Betsey, how does it feel? What are you going through?" I told her she didn't have to answer if she didn't want to.

But my experience is that most people are afraid to ask about the hard stuff. Yet it is often the hard stuff that we most need to talk about and to be unburdened from. Betsey was so relieved to talk about her elephant in the room; she wanted to be asked. She told us, "I feel tired sometimes, and I'm afraid because I don't know how the end is going to be and what I'm going to put my family through."

She talked all about it, and at the end she said, "Thank you for asking."

Sometimes the greatest comfort we can be for another person is to not ignore their needs or their fears, but to ask about them. And then to do our best to really listen.

Chapter 30

THE PINE BOX

When we bought Blackberry Farm, the property already had an old cemetery sitting below a thick tree line on a small rise next to a farm field. I knew when I died, I wanted to be buried at Blackberry. There was only one problem: two main Blackberry trails ran right past the exisiting cemetery. Golf carts were always coming and going on the pavement, and I couldn't imagine lying in that spot of ground and getting my eternal rest. I searched for another graveyard and a place to build a chapel while I was at it, until I found just the spot, next to a giant old beech tree, on the other side of a thin ribbon of Hesse Creek that runs through Blackberry. I had plans for a white clapboard chapel with a small plot to the side. When the beech limbs weren't rustling, I could hear the faint flutter of the creek, or at least I could hear it back then. Later, when we had the land studied, we learned that centuries before it had been an Indian burial ground.

And if I was going to be buried, I would need a coffin.

I was forty years old when I asked my favorite cabinetmaker

to make me a coffin. L. C. Jones was a beautiful woodworker, and I remember when I went to see him and said, "L.C., I gotta ask you something—will you build my casket?" His eyes welled up, and he couldn't say anything. I laughed and told him, "Don't worry. I'm well, I'm real well." I knew it was an unusual request, but I also knew I wanted it built right, and L.C. would do it better than anyone. He ordered the pine from Pennsylvania, and I told him that if he was making one, he might as well make two, because I assumed one day Sandy and I would be buried side by side. L.C. built the caskets and then he built boxes to protect them and stored them in his shop until he dismantled his storage space. Then I moved the caskets to the upper floor of Blackberry's old storage barn.

Sam told me once that employees and sometimes kids would climb up in the barn and take turns lying in my coffin. It was a joke of sorts. Until the last days of February 2016, when a couple of strong men carried my pine casket down from the rafters and out of that barn.

Mary Celeste was at a gas station filling up her car with little Sam when she got the call. Sam had skied into a pole on the intermediate trail during his first downhill run. No one had seen it happen. I was standing in the kitchen of my little Knoxville house, cooking lamb. My friend Brenda had dropped by; she wanted to go out for dinner and I wanted to stay in. My phone rang and the light flashed, I saw Mary Celeste's name on the caller ID.

It always stuns me how often the before and after in our lives is cleaved by the ring or now the buzz of a phone. Sandy Beall calling me at work to invite me on a date, Hunter Security call-

ing on a frigid February night about Rose Bay, a single text notification on the screen of Sandy's cell.

"Hey, Mary Celeste," I began. I could barely understand her;
all I heard was sobbing. I thought I heard her say, "Sam is dead,"
but I knew that couldn't be right. I put the phone on speaker so
Brenda could listen in and help me understand. But I had heard
it right the first time. Mary Celeste asked me to come to her
house to help tell the younger children. Brenda wanted to drive
me, but I refused. All those years of two cars, all the things I
have driven to and driven away from alone. She followed me,
hovering behind my speeding taillights and reckless turns. From
the road, she called Doug and several of my friends.

I knew Mary Celeste had told Cameron and Sam as soon as
she had arrived home. The three younger girls, Rose, Josephine,
and Lila still didn't know. They were waiting with the family
babysitter, Catherine, in the basement playroom. I will never
face a more agonizing walk than the one I took to descend that
set of ordinary stairs.

We gathered together on the sectional and Mary Celeste
managed to hold back her own grief to tell the unthinkable to
her children. I still don't recall her exact words, but what is
seared into my memory are the wails that followed.

Lila, age three, looked at her siblings, and then asked, "Why
is everybody so sad?"

Josephine answered, half-choking, "'Cause Daddy isn't coming home."

"Yes," Lila said back in that determined way of three-year-
olds, "Daddy's skiing. He's coming home."

We all wanted Lila to be right. How could it be that their
father, my son, would never come home again? That he would
never walk through the doors of that house and greet his chil-

dren after returning from a trip. Only twenty-four hours ago, I had watched him sitting at the end of the table, talking with his grandfather. Now he was gone.

Mary Celeste's best friend, Lynn, and her husband had raced over, and then Doug arrived. I remember him on the phone, making calls, trying to find out about what was needed to release Sam's body and have it returned to Knoxville. Then he prayed with us. Cameron retreated to her room, on her bed, with her Bible open. Sandy arrived sometime after eleven; he had gotten the last flight from New York. Around one a.m., I knew I had to go home. Again, I insisted on driving. My friend Meg followed me to my house, made sure I got inside, and offered to stay, but I didn't want anyone around. I felt an intense craving to be completely alone. I took off my shoes and got in bed with my clothes still on. Meg tiptoed down the stairs and locked the door, and I let the silence envelop me in thick layers. For the first time in thirty-nine years, six months, and four days, I was breathing on this earth without my eldest son.

When I came down the next morning, Brenda was waiting in my kitchen.

People started flowing in. Long-time friends Cathy and Matt came from Mobile. Camille and her daughter Hill were already in Nashville for a wedding; they came. My dear circle of women, Sharon, Dee, and Brenda opened their houses to anyone from out-of-town so everyone had a place to stay. In those first seventy-two hours, it was the aura of friendship that held me up, like an unbending line of steadying hands.

The Smoky Mountains are far enough south that the trees lining their peaks are largely deciduous and, once heavy with leaves, they breathe. On their exhale, they release not only oxygen but billowing clouds of organic compounds, creating their smoky haze. The Cherokee called this area alternatively the Great Blue Hills of God and the Land of Blue Smoke, and many mornings, the entire region is blanketed in a dense, opaque fog. Planes can't land, cars can only crawl, and there is nothing to do but wait for the light from above to slowly penetrate and the air and the ground to warm. For me, those early days after Sam died remain shrouded in a perpetual fog punctuated by sharp, bright-light memories. I see everyone gathered at Sharon Pryse's tall redbrick home. I can't remember the food or the flood of people, just the buzzing of conversation and then the sudden sharp image of Sharon's two petite side chairs and Sam and Mary Celeste's little Lila and Isabella, David and Lauren's daughter. The girls were three and two and they were carrying the small, low chairs from room to room, sitting briefly, then picking them up and moving on. Every bereavement should have little children with sticky hands, who play and run and laugh and jump and twirl and roll in the face of crushing sadness.

Saturday was spent planning the funeral. Doug and Mary Celeste's older sister, Muriel, had asked about the service, and Mary Celeste turned to me and said, "I'll do anything you want to do." Then someone else said, "Well, Kreis, what do you want to do?"

I had been to so few funerals. The only family one I could remember was Mammy's, nearly thirty years before. Surely there had to have been others, but Sandy and Kreis weren't good about going to weddings or funerals. Now I go to every one.

What I did have was forty years of experience planning things, and I knew I needed to see the sanctuary space again. I went to Cedar Springs Church with Camille and Suzanne, and some of the team in Blackberry's floral department. But rather than think about what would guests want, as I've always done,

I stood in that hushed sanctuary and thought, *What would Sam want?* The answer was clear: nothing artificial, only natural, seasonal things, living things. All the little things. The casket stand should be wood, not metal. There should be no flowers forced from trays in hot, humid greenhouses, only Lenten roses, his favorite flower, and vines, which were just beginning to show in the slowly thawing late February ground. And trees—there should be trees, like the forests Sam loved. We decided to line the stage with beech trees, which hold their leaves in the winter, clinging to the memory of the warm sun and steady rains of last year's growing season. Beech trees that had been growing in the forests on Blackberry's grounds, trees Sam would have passed from the time they were shaky, determined little saplings. The Blackberry team went into the woods and chose each beech, looking for the straightest and truest ones we could find. Then the farm's crew hand-dug the root balls, gently raising them from the cold ground.

Sam would also need clothes. Sandy, Mary Celeste, little Sam, and I were the ones who stood in his closet among his twelve bicycle helmets and fifty or more pairs of shoes—he was on his feet so much that he developed deep attachments to a variety of shoes—all neatly arranged, to pick out the last things he would ever wear, the shirt and pants and jacket that we would bury him in. His shoes, the helmets, the shirts, so many had a story, or reminded us of Sam. I looked at a pair of lace-up leather shoes and thought of the time that he had come home from Blackberry and I had talked about where I'd seen a flock of wild turkeys and how a wild turkey would be perfect for Thanksgiving. Without even changing his shoes, he went and got his shotgun. His children clamored to go and he said yes, but they had to wait and watch from the car. He was back fifteen minutes later, two long-necked wild turkeys swinging in his hands. Now there would never be another Thanksgiving with Sam.

We still didn't have Sam's body to bury. When there's been an accident it takes time for the coroner to release the remains. There are reports to complete and paperwork to file. Bureaucracy trumps burial. Grief is somehow required to be stamped and certified. Doug was the one who handled it; he knew whom to call and what strings to tug on. Ultimately, we found our answer in the kindness of a friend at FedEx who cut through red tape and made the difficult arrangements to bring Sam home on a transport plane. I remember standing in Hedgerose when Doug called to tell me that Sam's body was on a flight landing outside the cargo hanger at the TAC airport. The plan was for Sandy, David, and me to meet Sam, and I told Sandy to wait for David and me. Because I could not let my son, whose first cries I had never gotten to hear inside the obstetric operating room, come home this one last time without his mom.

When we arrived at the airport, Sandy, Doug, and the plane were lined up on the tarmac. It was dark and cold except where the harsh overheads splashed bright light on the black asphalt. The funeral home hearse had already pulled up alongside, and a young undertaker, still in her thirties, stood patiently off to the side. She extended her hand and said, "Hi, I'm Meg. I'll be taking care of Sam." I looked at her blankly and asked what that meant. "I'll be fixing him up," she explained.

I know in my mind that every day, somewhere, a parent meets the body of their child. But there is nothing to prepare you to meet your own son, wrapped and still, as he is wheeled down on a narrow gurney. He was bundled in a dark blanket, the corners tightly tucked and folded, and secured with two straps, one at the top and another at the bottom. Beneath, we could see the outlines of his long, lean form. It was the last flight he would ever take, the last time he would touch down in Tennessee. There would never be another journey home.

I would never again watch my son stand over the grill at a family dinner, lift up a squealing Lila, see the look of pride on his face when he talked about Blackberry, or see him hop off his bike, ruddy faced and sweat covered from trying to outrace the wind. Our circle of life had closed. This tarmac would be the last time that the four of us would come together on the same patch of earthly ground. As Doug said a prayer, Sandy, David, and I stepped forward and laid our hands on Sam. I took his foot.

All I could think was how stiff that foot felt in my hand. A dead body is so hard.

The prayer ended. We could do nothing except let go and watch as his body was loaded into the hearse. Then the door closed, the wheels rolled forward, and he was gone.

Mary Celeste's older sister, Muriel, her best friend, Lynn, and I were the ones who went to the funeral home. Meg told us that she had decided to go into the funeral business after her own mother died, and she asked questions about Sam, as if he were still living. I told her to take special care of his hair. Sam, with his mop of wild Beall family curls, had spent years searching for ways to tame his hair.

The church was just as we had wanted it, everything cleared out except for the nine big twenty-foot beech trees, one casket, and more than a thousand people. I felt my throat catch the moment I walked in. Lovingly, since early that morning, the Blackberry team had made everything beautiful for Sam, down to the perfect knots in the twine that bound the burlap wrap to the beech tree roots. The farm's dog handler had meticulously tied each one. The Lenten roses that covered the casket had a perfect bell shape and just the right balance of delicate flowers and sturdy green leaves. So many small signs of life in the midst of overwhelming loss.

I don't even know how all the guests knew about the funeral or knew where to come, but people had traveled from all over the world to be there with us on that morning. A thousand souls breathing in unison, wiping away tears together, and even occasionally laughing as one. A thousand voices joining together in prayer and song. Each of them was someone who cared about Sam.

Doug's own voice broke as he began the service. He spoke about how our family had "created safe places for people to laugh and weep and to be loved," and then he asked, "May you let us care for you today." Robbie Ventura, Sam's close friend from cycling, spoke about "Sam time," Sam's long pauses, his habit of ordering an entire menu for friends so that each person could taste everything. Sam truly did live life to the fullest. He liked the best of everything, and he gave the best of himself. Cameron read a letter to her dad: "You always had the biggest excitement for life." She added, "You never cared about me missing school for a good adventure because it would be a great memory." And she quoted from the Prophet Isaiah, who said, "The Lord of Hosts will prepare a lavish banquet for everyone on this mountain." To her father, Cameron said, "You were the perfect picture of God's love in the way that you cared for everyone so well."

Before the service started, Mary Celeste, Cameron, and I had been in the ladies' room and Mary Celeste said she thought she would speak. With no notes, she got up and told all of us, "I'm so thankful that Sam didn't waste his time." When she'd ask him, "Can we have normal?" Sam's reply was "That would be boring." She added that there was not one thing that Sam had not taught his children. They would be "great cooks, great athletes, hardworking, great lovers who love their family." She ended by talking about the "giant room and world of people who love you, and we're going to be okay." In Sam's words that he said each day to his family, "We're going to make it a great day."

Doug's final prayer was to ask God to "teach us to number our own days, to give our hours and minutes to what matters. If there's a relationship that needs to be reconciled, words of affection that need to be given and shared, may we give that and do that to honor Sam's life. May the healing begin." And then we followed Sam's vine-draped casket out of the sanctuary. He was going to be buried at Blackberry.

There was an old Blackberry tradition of waving off departing guests, where everyone lined up on the veranda and raised a white linen napkin. It was known as the Blackberry salute. On this afternoon, our Blackberry family lined the road waving their white linen napkins as Sam's casket passed. It was being pulled by a team of horses. The drivers were the same carriage drivers who led the wagon rides for guests around Blackberry every day. John and Carla had been Blackberry's neighbors since Sam had come back to run the farm. They wanted their horses to carry him one last time.

So they did, down the hill from the first house, around past the pond and the boathouse, and the Maple Cottage, and then beyond, to Hedgerose and the Shed. It was just past that spot, my once and always place of refuge, where Sandy, David, and I and the rest of the family were waiting to follow him. It had grown cloudy and dark and there was a brief spurt of rain, but what followed as we walked up the gravel road and toward the small chapel was a glistening rainbow, a Sambow, we said.

After more prayers, there was nothing left except to stand on the patch of grass and watch as the casket was lowered into the ground. The rest of the family filed off while Sandy, David, and I remained behind. We were the last ones to place the earth on Sam, ashes to ashes, dust to dust. The shovel set down, the three of us walked back to the main house together, the place where baby Sam had busied himself in his kitchen playpen and toddled out to serve guests in his footie pajamas. The place of so many memories that I did not even know I was making.

Chapter 31

TEARS AND LETTERS

The night Sam died, Cameron sat on her bed and opened her Bible, looking for comfort. She found a set of verses in Isaiah 25: 6–8: "On this mountain the Lord of hosts will make for all peoples a feast of rich food, a feast of well-aged wine, a rich food full of marrow, of aged wine well refined. And he will swallow up on this mountain the covering that is cast over all peoples, the veil that is spread over all nations. He will swallow up death forever; and the Lord God will wipe away tears from all faces . . ." Doug quoted these lines during Sam's funeral, saying that Isaiah is envisioning a heaven where people gather together amid a great mountain retreat. They share a table and enjoy the finest wines and the best meats, which sounds very much like what Sam had worked to build at Blackberry. In this one verse, he added, Cameron could be reminded both of Heaven and of her dad.

Sam may not have known it, but every time he welcomed someone into his home or prepared a meal, he was offering that person a glimpse of a fellowship beyond mere food or the passing of a few hours. It was a reminder to stop and appreciate life, to savor the moment and what you have shared. We did just that after Sam was laid to rest. I can see all of us inside Blackberry, the dining room and the living room lit up, and the pouring of wine and champagne and celebrating and eating, so like the feast on the mountain in Isaiah and such a beautiful picture of Heaven, where everyone comes together.

Life does go on. The next night, Sandy, David, and I did something we had not done in more than a decade: the three of us had dinner together and talked. We sat on the sofa in the living room at Blackberry, just as we had done when Sam was a restless toddler and David was a newborn, or on all those family Christmases, in our pajamas, surrounded by wrapping paper and stockings. And when we talked, it was not the false talk of politeness but a real conversation. It was as if Sam was still our family patriarch, bringing us to his table and making us feel at home. It wasn't a fix, but it was a start. If you don't start, you have no hope of moving forward.

The world did not stop because Sam died. If anything, the next weeks and months were like a snowball rolling downhill, gathering layers, gaining momentum. All five children had spring break plans, and those plans were going to be kept. Mary Celeste took Cameron on her senior trip; Sandy took Sam; Josephine and Lila went to Mary Celeste's mom in Mobile; and I had Rose. I went through the motions of fun, I played the part of grandmother, and I willed my eyes to stay dry. But at night, when I drifted off to sleep and in the morning when I woke, my last and first thoughts were always of Sam. At the end of the break, the family came together again for a long-planned baptism.

So on March 26, four weeks and one day after Sam died,

Rose, Josephine, and Lila were baptized. The ceremony was held in the little white Blackberry chapel, twenty feet from Sam's grave, with its new headstone and freshly planted Lenten roses lovingly brought from Sam and Mary Anne Beall's garden. Doug performed the service, speaking of hope and rebirth as he anointed their heads. Afterward, Mary Celeste and the children took photos, and it was one of the saddest, most beautiful things I have ever seen. Mary Celeste has always been good about marking milestones and taking photos. Now imagine taking your first family pictures without Daddy there, where his presence is marked by a modest gray stone.

The next morning, Easter Sunday, I was in Cashiers, North Carolina, to be with my friends Sharon and Joe. We went to the local Episcopal church and I broke almost as soon as I reached the pew. I wept the entire service, not little tears, but big, dripping sobs. It was a physical grief unlike anything I have ever known, a body-shaking grief, as if I were a tiny boat being pitched and tossed by waves of sadness breaking over me one by one. It was as if, away from the immediate needs of my family and surrounded by reminders of death and holy resurrection, I could finally grieve my son. My faith was my ballast. In the message and the meaning of that Easter morning, Jesus seemed to wrap his arms around my private grief. My friends and the compassion of complete strangers in that congregation were my anchor, my lifeline. They righted me. And going forward, my faith was what gave me a sure foot on which to stand. I will never understand Sam's death, but at the same time, I have never been more sure of my faith or more grateful for the rough and winding path that led me to the Lord.

Before and after the tears came the letters. They came from friends, from strangers, from Blackberry guests who wrote with remembrances of Sam's kindness or a special moment they shared. I got letters from mothers who had also buried their children, a sorority of loss that none of us expects to join. The cards and letters were like so many hands holding mine, telling me I was not alone.

Except for one letter that said simply, "I was sorry to hear of the loss of your son Sam." It was signed "David Bailey." Even knowing that my father was in full-on decline, that letter still sat like a scar on my heart.

In April, I went back to Blackberry to work full time as director of design, a position I would keep for the next year, until it was time to turn the job over to someone younger, to another generation. In those months, I tried to do what I knew best: keep the public home that Sam had poured his soul into, where he had created his own feast on the mountain, beautiful. Before he died, Sam had plans for a large wine cellar to run underground from the dining room at the Barn out to a new gathering building we named Bramble Hall. It was his elegant solution to a substantial problem for a food and wine destination—for a few years, he had been forced to use a climate-controlled tractor-trailer wine storage unit—but it was more. He wanted it to be underground so none of the staff would have to go outside in bad weather and also to create ideal conditions for storage so that he could preserve the small batches of wine made by his vintner friends, respecting their craft as they respected his. It was buried deep, and invisible from the outside, like so much in Sam. It was never just a wine cellar; it was thinking in so many directions, it was symbolic of all the ways he poured his heart and soul into Blackberry. He wanted what was best for Blackberry, no matter how lofty, in much the same way that I had wanted the best, but also in his own "Sam" way, with his own vision.

When it was completed, so many times I would sit in the dining room at the Barn and look out over everything, and it was as if I could still feel his presence, appreciate his touches of creativity. There were times when it felt joyous, sensing these bits of Sam, and times when I felt my throat catch and my eyes well up and I could not fully explain how sitting at a table in a beautiful room made me want to cry.

I also turned a portion of the old barn, where the caskets had once been stored, into my office. It was the oldest part of the farm, adjacent to the Shed, and it seemed like the best place to draw future inspiration and to keep that spark of our family and my son. The poet Zachry Douglas put it so well when he wrote,

the broken will always be
able to love harder than
most.

once you have been in the
dark, you learn to
appreciate everything
that shines.

Now when I walk down the small road that runs beside the Shed and the remodeled barn, so many times I find myself taking the longer route, bearing left along the gentle curve by the creek, crossing the narrow bridge, and taking the path that circles past the little church with its white square fence, plot of green grass, and patch of Lenten roses. From there, my eyes gaze upon a simple carved stone, beneath which rests my Sam.

Chapter 32

VISITING

We have each found our own ways to be with Sam.

The October after he died, when the trees were still lit with color but each wind brought a few more leaves to the ground, my nearly four-year-old granddaughter, Lila, decided to go for a walk. She left me sitting on my porch at Hedgerose as she trotted off in bare feet, pushing her baby doll, Ellie, in her little pink stroller. I watched as she passed through the empty field that runs from my house down to Hesse Creek. The grass was wet, but that only made her push harder, the pint-size stroller's little wheels weaving a fresh irregular trail. When she got to the fence line, she turned and called out at the top of her lungs, "Do you need me?"

I smiled, waved, and answered, "No." She pushed Ellie a few more yards, paused, and called again, "Do you need me?" I smiled and shook my head no until she said, "Well, I need you."

With those words, I was off, in my bare feet. Lila grinned as I caught up to her, as if she had known my true answer all along. At first she wanted me to climb with her on tree stumps, but after a few minutes she returned to her mission. "Just follow me," she instructed. So I followed as we doubled back along the gravel path, the pea-size rocks stinging the bottom of my feet. I quickly retreated to the grass while Lila kept going over the rocks, undeterred, pushing her stroller onward, its wheels clacking against the stones. Soon we crossed Hesse Creek at the covered bridge and turned left, the same route I had walked six months before, following behind Sam's casket. "Hey, Lila," I asked, "where are we going?"

"Just follow me. Just follow me. Just follow me." By now I saw the chapel coming into view. "We are going to say hi to my daddy."

She opened the double doors and instructed me to take a seat in a pew while she read a story. Holding up the Bible, she began, "There once was a boy named Doug. That is what this place is called—Doug Banister. He came here once because my daddy died. The end." Then Lila left the small, plain sanctuary and headed to the bench under the tree that overlooks Sam's grave. She scooped up her baby doll, placed her on the bench, sat down, and patted the wood for me to join her. Side by side, we gazed upon that single tombstone until Lila picked up her doll and stood, signaling it was time to go. In her clear, purposeful voice, she said, "Bye, Daddy."

We walked back just as we had come, along the path, across the bridge, and through the field, to the door of my house, the first house that Sam and Mary Celeste had lived in when they began their lives at Blackberry Farm.

Another year passed and as the leaves began to turn, Mary Anne Beall lay dying. She was in the hospital on a breathing machine, and at one point she opened her eyes, saw all the family assembled, and asked, "Am I at my wake?" For her last day of consciousness, she came home. She had made a list of family and friends she wanted to see, and she asked for me to come in the morning. She looked at me and said, "Kreis, I'm going to be with Sam soon." In those words was the full circle of life, embracing both living and loss as two inseparable strands. We buried her in the chapel graveyard near her grandson. And when her husband, Sam, says grace or prayers, he addresses his words to "God and Mary Anne."

Two more seasons passed, and in the summer of 2018, Sandy and I were together at Blackberry for a series of meetings. After everyone had left, I returned to drop off some papers and found Sandy sitting there. I had planned to drive by the new homes and buildings under development and I asked Sandy if he wanted to come along. We looked at the construction and then I said, "Sandy, let's go visit Sam."

We rode in the cart to Sam's grave. Sometimes, when the time is right, you can ask things. In more than two years, I had never asked him for the details of Sam's death. I had not been strong enough to hear them. Now I was. As Sandy spoke, I listened, and for the first time, I saw Sandy cry for our son. He shared something else, too. He told me how in 2012, around the time of our divorce, Sam had upset him. He thought Sam was neglecting his wife and his family, being short in conversation, taking them for granted. Just as his father had done for the two of us, Sandy sat down and wrote Sam and Mary Celeste a letter, telling his son to do better. "It could have just as easily been us that you wrote about," I said to Sandy. "Do you know that there were times when you were much the same with me?" He agreed and said that he could see that now.

And then I thought about Sam's decision to go home each night to cook dinner for his children, about our Friday lunches, about his words "I want to know you, Mom."

On the ruins of my marriage, I was given the gift of getting to know my son. Sam's children were given the gift of a present father, and Mary Celeste was given the gift of purposeful time before time ran out. Sam did what so many of us fail to do: he changed. Did Sandy's and my marriage have to implode to receive those gifts? That will always be unknowable, but the simple truth is we received them and we were able to live them. They were gifts given in the light of the moment, when we could not know what darkness lay in the future. I will never understand Sam's death, but I can give thanks for the ways in which we all had a chance to do better and live better before that moment came.

I think about my son every day, but in that suffering, I catch glimpses of goodness and light and love. I often go back to the biblical story of Joseph and his brothers, a story of Joseph's hubris, believing that he was better than his siblings because he was the one most doted upon by his father, of his brothers' anger and how they threw him into a dry well and then sold him into slavery, forcing him from his homeland in Canaan down to Egypt, even faking his death. There are so many verses recounting animosity, deceit, and betrayal, but always underneath there is the pull of family that bound them together and eventually reunited them. Each character was imperfect, yet each persevered and endured. The Bible also tells us that God was always with Joseph, no matter what his imperfections. And in the end, what did Joseph wish for? That his bones be returned to Israel so that he might be buried at home. It was Moses who honored that wish and carried Joseph's remains on the exodus out of Egypt. That this story has endured for so many years speaks to the powerful pull of and longing for family and home.

But it is also the story of how everyone in that family was afraid to speak their truths. Joseph's brothers were afraid to say how they really felt, so they sold their brother into slavery and pretended he was dead. When, years later, Joseph saw his brothers in Egypt, he was afraid to tell them right away who he was. Everyone made up ruses and fabrications; each person withheld something of themselves. How often, though, do we do that in our own lives? How many years did I do that even in my own family?

I cannot go back and change what happened in the past. The only thing I can do is to learn to grow in the present. After we visited Sam's grave, Sandy and I went back to the original dining room at Blackberry to have dinner. I finally asked him the question that I could not ask for so many years: "Sandy, why did we get a divorce?" He answered, "That is a good question, and I'll send you an email." This time, he did. In part, what he wrote was "We were both hard-headed, opinionated, needless to say didn't always agree but those strong wills and opinions (painful through the process sometimes) added to creating the special and sometimes the magic. Neither one of us could have done all we did without the other. We were a team and it consumed our life—the positive and the negative of our married life. We have both grown beyond most of our craziness, still friends and partners in many ways." And it is true. We have journeyed to a place where we can both say, *We are sorry.*

Each day, I try to learn from the past, live for the future, and embrace the present. I want to be a better mother and grand-mother, a better friend, a more compassionate person. To truly live in a new home that is defined by more than its walls. To let love for my family shine again. That is how I can honor all of my family and both of my sons.

PEACE

I have done so many things wrong, but I have done three things right: I have birthed my two sons and Blackberry Farm. I always thought I loved houses, but what I truly love is home, the place where we are loved, known, and safe. The place we seek to return to over and over again, or the place we spend much of our lives trying to find.

Blackberry Farm will always be my home. It is the place that held me, comforted me, and whispered reminders to me of who I am when I was lost and had forgotten. Blackberry is the place where my children began their lives, where my grandchildren have splashed in the creek and dug in the ground, and where three of them were baptized within sight of their father's grave. I sit here, exactly where I started, although I am not the same woman I was forty years ago. I learned in the Shed that it is not the size of the space but the depth of the person in it. Those four walls are a place I have returned to, to laugh and to cry, to sit with pain but also with joy. Because a home is so much more than the physical structure of a house. To me, home is God, family, friends, and legacy. A house is a building; a home is a heart. It is love, people, relationships, and the life you live in it.

Acknowledgments

My first thank-yous are to my family:

Mom—Where do I begin? Mom, you showed me beauty, you taught me independence and grace. Any success I have known began with you—I could not and would not have wanted to do it without you, Mom.

David—For marching to the beat of your own drum so beautifully. You have always been so true and authentic to who you are. You've been there for me when I have needed you most. You are the kindest and most genuine son a mother could ever hope for and I am so proud of who you are, Dave.

Sam—You asked me the most important question a family member has ever asked me when you said, "Mom, I want to know you. What's important to you?" We all want to be known. I'm so thankful to you that we had started the incredible journey.

Sandy—To the first person who ever believed in me. Our thirty-six years were never boring and they still aren't. We worked hard and together created so much magic in our years together. We gave far more to our work than to our marriage. Sorry, Sandy.

Mary Celeste and Lauren—To my beautiful daughters-in-law, thank you for loving my sons and for surviving all that our family requires, and giving back more than I could have ever hoped for. Sam and David could not have chosen better wives and mothers for your children. I love you both so much.

To my grandchildren: Cameron, Sam, Rose, Josephine, Lila, Isabella, and Stella—You are my wonderful, loving sorority, plus my one lone boy. Thanks for all our adventures. You bring your Yaya more joy than you will ever know.

Mammy—You were always there for us, I knew I could count on you. You taught me humility in giving. You were consistent and stable, everything a grandmother is supposed to be and you emulated "the answer is yes, what's the question," for us.

Keith—To my big sister. We have certainly both come a long way, and your friendship, love, and support mean more than you will ever know. Thanks for always telling me the truth and being willing to call me out when I am being a real jerk.

Abby and Dylan—I'm the luckiest aunt in the world to have had the privilege of being in your lives and watching you grow up. I'll never forget our ongoing and meaningful dinner conversations—a house with four boys makes for some "colorful" commentary.

Mary Anne Beall (Non)—You showed me how to live and you showed me how to die. Thank you for being the guiding and gracious matriarch of our Beall clan.

Sam Beall (Pop)—You are the head of our family, our leader by being a great father, grandfather, great-grandfather, and best ex-father-in-law.

The Olsen family—Thanks for reaching out with love to me, the untouchable, and for sharing holidays with unmatched graciousness. I am so blessed to share our lives and our granddaughters.

The entire Beall family—Thanks for the memories. You all have loved me and welcomed me over the years and I am grateful to each and every one of you that together, we are family.

Kim—To my little sister with the biggest heart who is sweet to the bone. You dance like an angel and you are amazing.

Louis Nelson—Thank you for wearing the badge of devotion to Kim through thick and thin. Your love is healing.

Thank you to my wonderful book team:

Lyric Winik—Thank you for somehow putting my story into words. You deserve all the gold stars in heaven for your patience and for somehow managing to organize my thoughts and put them in readable terms. You pulled the essence to the point where I cried nearly every time I finished my own book, even though I knew my own story! You are a beautiful crafter of words and I am forever grateful to you for bringing my story to life.

Grainne Fox, my agent—Thank you for being my cheerleader, my advocate, and for believing in my story. Your Irish wit, humor, and of course, your thoughtful guidance made this process more than just a "lick off the old Blarney stone."

Christy Fletcher, Fletcher & Co.—For seeing the promise in this story and for your generosity and unwavering support.

At Crown/Convergent: Mary Reynics, my editor—Your intellect and discernment make my voice stronger and more precise than on my own. Thank you.

Tina Constable, my publisher—I could not ask for a more welcoming or supportive publishing house, especially the support of **Campell Wharton, Andrea DeWerd, Cindy Murray.**

The jacket design team, led by **Jesse Sayward Bright.**

The publicity team, led by **Cindy Murray,** and the rest of the Crown family.

Ashley Hong—Thank you for your help.

And to the Crown security guard, thanks for not giving me the boot when this country girl came to town and started snapping pictures of the book walls because she didn't know she wasn't allowed to.

Matt Ferebee—Thank you for the fifteen years of inspiration and friendship. You know me and my voice, thank you for your humble spirit and guiding creativity.

Velda Hughes—Thanks for being an "original" like me. God help us. Your tenacity and grit inspire me every day.

Jo Shuffler—For quick turnarounds and outstanding attention to detail.

Molly Teas, Jim Wallwork, and **Jean Sheeleigh**—For their very careful reads.

Thank you to my dear friends and guides in my life:

Doug Banister—You were the person I could be vulnerable with. You are my guide who met the wounded Kreis, listened, gave me a plan, and who continues to steer me in the right direction through success and failure. You have been steadfast and constant. Thank you.

Meg Davis—Nobody knows me better than you. We are unlikely best friends. We laugh, dance-write, and pray. Together we lean into the mess, accept the challenge, and push to be our best. Knowing you is one of the greatest blessings in my life. I am here for you, always.

Teresa Dunn—For giving me the tools and the language I needed to meet myself. Thank you for pushing me and keeping me in "healthy reality."

Bernadette Doyle—For being my "memory," my friend, and for living through it all. For knowing things that nobody else dare ever know.

John Fleer—You are an incredible man who went beyond your job description. Blackberry Farm owes a great deal of debt to you—we would not be where we are today without you. Thank you for your leadership and your friendship.

Camille Luscher—For being my like-soul friend who is always teaching me. Nobody exemplifies the art of living more than you. And thank you for always allowing me to invite myself over.

Hayes, Hebard, and Hill Luscher—Thanks for letting me be Miss Kreis to you all over the years. You feel like my second set of children and I have loved getting to watch you grow up and become the fabulous adults you are now.

Cathy Mosteller—For being the kindest, most compassionate person I have ever known. What wisdom and care you endlessly offer. I aspire to be like you when I grow up.

Matt Mosteller—Matt, you are one of the great men in my life as well as one of my biggest inspirations. You have been to hell and back and continue to show the world what it looks like to journey through pain with humility and grace.

Thresia—I don't know where to start. You are the glue that has held my life together with kindness, love, and genuine giving. You've watched my back from the beginning. I am humbled forever by your loyalty.

Franklin—Thank you for always being there wherever you are needed and gladly taking care of all the details.

Brenda—You are my safe and constant friend, an angel in my life. You are fiercely loyal. Thanks for being willing to break out the "ball bat" when needed.

Sharon/Joe—Thanks for letting me be in your sidecar with a microphone and for spending the "non-eymoon" together at Phantom Ranch.

Karen Brooks—Thanks for hugging me with knowing eyes.

Dee—Nobody in the world knows me like you do, the first person I call in a disaster. You are a trusting, powerful, and giving friend.

Suzanne Kasler—Thanks for keeping my world beautiful and for being my friend who tells me (most) of the truth. You know all the highs and lows of my work and personal life in a way no one else does . . . thanks for still being my friend.

Samantha Feuer—To my protégé of three wonderful years who took care of me as we grew together.

Leah Thompson—You are a wonderful, one-of-a-kind person. Three thousand miles and seven years later, I know that I can always count on you.

Lucy Schaad—Thanks for making my world a better place, with one call and many kind invitations of traveling, hiking, cooking, and of course, houses.

Tommie Rush and Richard Jolley—Thank you for your true gift of hospitality through your deep love of each other and the way that gives back to me and the world in so many ways. You inspire me every day and your friendship means so much.

Heather Anne Thomas Longo—To my phantom photography partner who is loyal and knowing with insightful and genuine love.

Monica Langley—Thank you for your wisdom and for showing me the way.

Caesar Stair—Thanks for being my coach, in the pool and in the courtroom.

Mary Holland—Our lives have paralleled and intersected for two dozen years when I needed you most.

Andy Saftel and Susan Knowles—Heartfelt love for our Pikeville picnics at your studio over the years, and capturing my family's soul on canvas—I am humbled by your quiet and constant love.

Chuck Alexander—For twenty-eight years, we built my dreams and grew our companies together—you made my world a better place one building at a time.

Keith Summerour—Thanks for designing many, many of my dreams.

John Hawker—Thank you for building the Shed, the home where I met God and me.

Susanne Hassell—Thanks for knowing me on my needy terms and breathing life into my soul.

Adella Thompson—It doesn't get better than sharing Jesus, family, and Sweet Baby James with you.

Susan Wojnar—Thanks for our pilgrimage together through work, church, dogs, and daffodils.

Sarah Brown—Your gift of prophecy is divine in your work and in our friendship. Thank you.

Cat Hedberg—You are my Earth Mother/Sister whose life-giving force has exemplified nurturing for thirty-plus years.

Helene and Steve Nichols—Thank you for being two rocks in my life who exemplify and embody the picture of true love.

Sarah Rau—To my talented and patient friend who exhibits grace everywhere.

Nan Sprouse—Thanks for keeping me strong in faith and being my inspirational wellness doctor.

Daryl Arnold—Thanks for giving new meaning to "sausage and eggs."

Carol Stewart—Thank you for writing me and telling me, "I want you in my life."

Ali and Charles Banks—You are two of the angels in my life. I am so grateful that our lives and families are so interwoven through all the joy and all the pain.

Dwight Tarwater—I am grateful that we both have the same boss, and with Him, our possibilities are endless.

My special gratitude to the Blackberry family—Thanks for making the dream come alive every day, letting me watch the heart go on. I am incredibly humbled by all the people that love this special place in Tennessee.

And finally, I would like to acknowledge my own failings and shortcomings, the biggest of them likely being this: I overshare, therefore I am. I am certain that I have a lot of sorries to say, so I'll just say one big fat **SORRY** to cover all my bases.

About the Author

Kreis Beall is the co-founder of Blackberry Farm, an award-winning Relais & Châteaux inn and resort in the Smoky Mountains of East Tennessee and one of the country's premier destinations. Entrepreneurial and artistic, Kreis brings her skills as a designer, home cook, inn proprietor, photographer, and adventurer to her passion for living. Her homes and design work have been featured in many leading shelter magazines, and she currently serves as Blackberry's Director of Design Emeritus. In addition to being a respected speaker, she is a long-term survivor of traumatic brain injury. Born and bred in Tennessee, Kreis is the mother of two sons and a grandmother of seven. When Kreis isn't speaking, writing, or renovating, you can find her riding in an RV on Route 66, hiking up mountains, or dancing in her kitchen as she cooks.

About the Type

This book was set in Garamond, a typeface originally designed by the Parisian type cutter Claude Garamond (c. 1500–61). This version of Garamond was modeled on a 1592 specimen sheet from the Egenolff-Berner foundry, which was produced from types assumed to have been brought to Frankfurt by the punch cutter Jacques Sabon (c. 1520–80).

Claude Garamond's distinguished romans and italics first appeared in *Opera Ciceronis* in 1543–44. The Garamond types are clear, open, and elegant.